Praise for *Scottish Independence: A Feminist Response*

"Accessible, fr
succinct book s
social history a
independence. I
is its new strate
Bridget Fowler, E
Glasgow

CW00816159

"In this timely and tightly argued book, Jenny Morrison and Cat Boyd argue that the situation of women will be a crucial test of how far Scotland has broken from the UK's dismal record in relation to democracy, equality and social justice. Regardless of whether Scotland becomes independent in the short-term or not, this is a serious contribution to both the ongoing debate and the literature of 'fourth-wave' feminism."
Neil Davidson, Senior Lecturer in Sociology, University of Glasgow

"This is a bracing and highly readable book that shows not only how women have suffered under the neoliberal madness of successive UK governments but how their lives can be transformed, and their freedoms extended, by the revolutionary potential of independence."
Alan Bissett

"A welcome contribution to the independence debate, a must read for feminists, trade unionists and all those who want an alternative to neoliberalism."
Sarah Collins, STUC Youth Committee (pc)

To Peggy, Marie, and Juliana

SCOTTISH INDEPENDENCE
A FEMINIST RESPONSE

CAT BOYD AND JENNY MORRISON

WP
BOOKS

WP
BOOKS

Published by Word Power Books 2014
Word Power Books
43-45 West Nicolson Street
Edinburgh EH8 9DB
www.word-power.co.uk

Designed and Typeset by James Foley and Sinead Dunn.

Printed in the UK by Print Domain, 107 High Street,
Thurnscoe, Rotherham, S. Yorks S63 0QZ.

British Library Cataloguing in Publication Data.
A catalogue record for this book is available from the
British Library.

ISBN: 978-0-9927392-4-9

CONTENTS

ACKNOWLEDGEMENTS

We wish to thank everyone who edited, proofread and contributed to this pamphlet: we couldn't have produced this in the three weeks in which we did without your help. Thank you to Sinead O'Donnell Dunn for the cover.

---1---

INTRODUCTION

> We're told independence will be better, but we need to know what "better" would look like. If things were just the same, what's the point?

On International Women's Day 2014, an article appeared on the independence blog, *Bella Caledonia*, quoting the unnamed woman above. Her words exactly express our intentions in this book. We do not consider ourselves experts on these topics, nor do we think that we have all the answers. This is not a political strategy, nor posturing to "win women" (that imagined homogenous group) to a Yes vote. Instead, as socialists, internationalists and feminists, we see independence as a means to transform society. We know that things cannot continue the way they are: something must change for women.

Britain is failing in many ways, and failing women in particular. We live in one of the most unequal countries in Europe. While the proportion of women in the UK who work is above the OECD average, the percentage holding full-time jobs is lower than in all but two other countries. The gender pay gap is one of the highest in Europe, and since 2000, the UK has been outstripped in terms of progress on all these issues. Westminster cannot reform this away: it results from a cross-party consensus for neoliberal policies that destroy the public sector and erode pay and conditions.

Women have even less reason than men to trust in the status quo, yet according to the polls are less likely than men to vote for independence. A typical round of misogynistic posturing has followed from both the Yes and No campaigns, explaining variously that women are "risk averse" or trying to appeal to "things women are interested in". Yet, when asked, women are interested in the same things as men: the economy, Trident and NATO, democracy and representation.

If the official Yes campaign fails, it's because of its gender blindness: they've failed to show how a Yes vote can transform the current consensus which creates and recreates inequality for women. We want a Scotland that is equal for all genders. But we can't achieve that without confronting the current relations of power in our society that privilege white, straight, rich men.

The question we want to answer is not whether Scotland should be an independent country, but how a Yes vote can change the lives of Scottish women. This is a case for radical change, which seeks to expose the current system and explain what "better" would look like. We don't want to see a post-Yes Scottish society that's simply more of the same.

Independence is by no means an automatic ticket out of the current neoliberal settlement in Britain. While there has been a rhetoric of gender equality in the Scottish Parliament, the Scottish Government, including under the SNP, has overseen a period of enhanced marketisation that pushes women into low-wage precarious work while reinforcing unpaid work in the care economy. A constitution for an independent Scotland that enshrines equality will mean very little if it bases itself on this economic model.

But a Yes vote throws the current consensus into the open and alternative possibilities can be explored.

A progressive case for independence is being discussed, particularly in the Common Weal initiative, launched by the Jimmy Reid Foundation, which aims to put Scotland on a path to Nordic citizenship. This concept is based on fairer social guarantees, a better standard of living and a shift in the gender settlement with some enhanced, and supported, rights for women. SNP councillors have unanimously backed the Common Weal vision, committing at least in rhetoric to social democracy, which gives some basis to hold them to account after an independence vote. Such a commitment, even if it turns out to be empty, would be out of bounds in Westminster.

But a problem exists in this vision: how much change would these reforms really provide if they are not willing to challenge the root of gender and class inequality in the neoliberal system itself? While we respect and support the egalitarian impulse of the gender contribution to the Common Weal initiative, we recognise its reliance on a benevolent political class that can quite comfortably grant certain populist left demands but will not challenge the inequality which is the basis for its own wealth and privilege. Scotland may be at an advantage to England in being able to gain concessions, but all the mainstreaming in the world won't improve much for most women if a neoliberal system underneath requires ever-increasing exploitation reliant on a sexual division of labour.

Feminism has sometimes been guilty of focusing too narrowly. In the turn to lobbying government, it has become attached to a declining system of unrepresentative institutions and its imagination has been constricted. Yet there exists the opposite danger: merely polemicising about patriarchy has its limits too. Independence is an opportunity to re-democratise, become a movement again. Feminism needs to engage with policies to improve life for women and attempt to push the boundaries of these visions. It is necessary to go beyond piecemeal reform and instead focus on increasing the collective power of women in society; particularly the power of working class and other marginalised women. We support small reforms, but we cannot remain complacent.

Independence can open subversive opportunities. The word "radical" has its origins in the word "root", and our intention when it comes to an independent Scotland is to pull up at the root the existing structures and institutions of domination. An independent Scotland that is a replica of a corrupt, imperialist neoliberal Britain provides nothing for the majority of women. We need a strong feminist radical movement that sets the agenda for the independence debate. We aim to start this debate with the arguments in this book.

Many of the ideas here draw from feminist projects, theories and imaginings; but we also draw from conversations and interactions with countless activists within the independence campaign. We have read other feminist publications engaging with independence with great interest, particularly the gender chapter of the Common Weal book, as we believe it is essential that women are at the centre of the independence project. However, we want to defend our own vision of radical change, one that goes deeper than surface policy changes to examine underlying structures.

This book was written in the opening weeks of July of this year. We don't argue that we have provided a definitive nor perfect blueprint for a feminist radical Scotland. But we hope that this is a contribution to opening up an important debate about the kind of independent Scotland that we want: one that counts women in.

---2---

HISTORY/HERSTORY

|| INTRODUCTION ||

It's a misogynist country…The reason why the Conservatives lost all their seats was because of Margaret [Thatcher], because she was a woman.

These comments, by ex-Tory cabinet minister Lord Young, typify the view that Scotland cannot accept women in politics. Leaving aside the many other good reasons why Scots dislike Thatcher, it is a strange point to make now, when women (one of them, Ruth Davidson, an open lesbian) lead two-of-three main Holyrood parties. And considering Nicola Sturgeon is the SNP's deputy leader and increasingly the party's public face, women arguably dominate Scotland's political leadership. By contrast, men lead all main Westminster parties, and this seems unlikely to change soon. Misogynistic attitudes to women in politics are rife across Britain: Scotland's problems are undeniable, but they are typical not exceptional.

True, Scotland does have a certain macho image; many glorify "traditions" of fighting, alcohol and sectarianism. Our national mythology ranges from strong, warrior clansmen and mysterious fey women through to the frontline-kilted Highland soldier or the wee Glasgow hard man. A physically-strong masculinity dominates, with hard northern men held up against soft English southerners. Yet such symbols have complex roots in British militarism and the industrial heritage of the British Empire. They are Scottish dimensions of a UK culture of war, imperialism and profit.

We should also be wary of an equally wrong-headed nationalist myth, which substitutes an egalitarian Scottish story in place of a distinctively misogynistic one. That Scotland is intrinsically more enlightened than elsewhere in Britain is inaccurate, or at best one-sided. The old tale, whereby strong Scots women dominate cowed men, where Clyde workers wouldn't dare bring home open pay packets to their wives, has little basis in historical fact. In fact, Scottish men notoriously squandered their wages *before* returning to their families. The trade unions even had to run campaigns to persuade pub landlords to stop serving men when they'd drunk half their pay. "Good men" returned home with wages unopened, but many lied about how much they earned.

Only a highly selective reading of history suggests a particularly egalitarian Scottish tradition for women. It asks us to forget Scottish women's conspicuous absence from key events, even in progressive accounts. The Scottish Enlightenment was even more male than the French, and Scotland never experienced a blossoming of women's debating societies as in France, or a Scottish version of Mary Wollstonecraft's *The Vindication of the Rights of Women*. We *can* uncover the strength and agency displayed by Scottish women in history, but not by denying Scotland's misogynistic legacy.

Such denials obscure the oppressive reality of life for Scottish women who, like women elsewhere in Britain, suffer some of the highest poverty, the lowest wages and the largest gender pay gap in Europe. Scotland has huge problems with oppression and patriarchy; but these reflect its similarities to Britain not its differences. Scotland is still too British, and this is why we need change. But in creating a new Scotland, we should be conscious of our own gendered history and mythology. Independence alone will not break with the misogyny past and present. Effective arguments for self-determination must have a feminist political consciousness.

|| Myths of Nation and Class ||

The privileging of men, and by extension symbols of masculinity, imbues the imagery and history of Scottish national identity. As with many European countries, Scotland represents itself as a female figure, Dame Scotia; but she less commonly embodies the nation than rivals such as Britannia, Marianne and Germania for Britain, France and Germany respectively. The association of the nation as the motherland – a gendered symbol of women and nation as home and bearers of culture – has been weaker in Scotland than elsewhere.

By contrast, symbols of masculinity, in particular the Highland militarism already noted, dominate the Scottish imagination. Celebrations of imperial tartanry remain part of our living culture today, with parades, warlike ceremonies and the Edinburgh Military Tattoo all designed to tie Scottish to the armed forces. Even the bagpipes, our national instrument, have a strong military connection and are often taught to school pupils by former soldiers.

Scotland's national heroes, from Wallace to Bruce to Scott, are almost entirely male, as are the collective of the clans who fought the Jacobites. There are occasional exceptions, Flora MacDonald being one of the most notable, but such figures are always placed within their own femininity. Although she was in reality a part of a slave owning society in North Carolina, she is promoted as the epitome of feminine virtue, honourable and dignified.

The independence debate has, to its credit, stayed away from the nationalist stereotypes of *Braveheart* and Wallace. However, instead it is pulling on an alternative myth of Scottish identity: that of an inherent Scottish egalitarianism and social democracy that varies from the left-wing of the SNP to the socialist left.

Yet, the heroes of the left, from Burns to Reid through to MacDiarmid and Maclean, are also exclusively male. Similarly, the focus is on large male dominated events such as Red Clydeside or the Upper Clyde Shipbuilders work-in. This is not to deny the importance of such events; but political action engaged in by women, especially beyond the established boundaries of trade union activism, is too often ignored.

Awareness has risen in recent times, so that most left-wing histories contain a chapter on women or aim to uncover the part played by significant women in history. But simply adding women does not address the gendered nature of national history. We need to develop a women's identity in Scotland, based not on nationalism but one with an internationalist reach and transformative potential.

|| WOMEN IN SCOTTISH HISTORY ||

Despite male dominance in much of Scotland's story, Scotland also has a proud history of women's self-organisation that can act as the basis for a Scottish feminist consciousness. Women have always organised and fought for recognition. An examination of recent Scottish history also belies the idea that a politics for all people is enough. Instead it shows that we need to fight specifically for women in order to create a better Scotland for us to all to live in. But also, it shows how Scottish women used campaigns for broader reform to extend their own rights.

In popular consciousness, feminist activism starts with the Suffragettes, but in reality women played a role throughout our industrial history. Chartism in Scotland, for instance, shows some of the contradictions between gender and class. This working class movement took its name from the People's Charter of 1838, which called for six main democratic reforms. At its height, millions from across Britain signed the petition, and many women were fully involved in the campaign. Yet despite some nods to women's rights, the Chartists focused on men and campaigns for a family wage so that women need not work. While women supported the Chartist message, they also went beyond it and began to introduce demands for their own rights. This saw the establishment of the first women's suffrage societies and the demand for a more active role in the movement.

Chartism declined in the 1850s but women's suffrage was increasingly taken up by liberal intellectuals and women's suffrage societies formed in most major cities in the 1860s and 70s. The Suffragettes of the Women's Social and Political Union (WSPU) formed in 1903 arguing for more militant action with the slogan "deeds not words". The WSPU was active across Britain but Scotland was a particular focus of militant campaigning. At the same time, Scottish Suffragettes had to emphasise their distinct identity when confronted with a London-centric campaign: for example, one of the key slogans against the Liberal government which refused to support the cause was "you maunna tramp on the Scots thistle laddie".

Whilst the Suffragettes were a cross-class movement, and there were tensions between the interests of upper class women who wanted equality with men of their own class and working class women who wanted reform across society, the energy of the movement fed into and out of other women's organisation. The Glasgow Rent Strikes of 1915 have been rightly lionised as a great moment of women's self-organisation and a crucial part of the Red Clydeside story. With the outbreak of war in 1914, landlords threatened steep rent rises; in response, women organised a payment strike. The leaders and promoters were suffrage activists.

The suffrage movement had partial success in 1918 with the Representation of the People Act which expanded the male suffrage and gave women over 30 the right to vote subject to property requirements. It was not until 1928 that women gained the right to vote on equal terms with men. Politics in this period became increasingly polarised on a class basis and there was recognition from the left of the need to appeal to women. While the energy and focus of the suffrage movement waned, women also continued to organise for the need to take women's specific economic and social rights into account. Yet this gained limited support from political parties, including those of the left.

|| THE MODERN PERIOD ||

In the sixties, as across Europe, "second wave" feminism emerged in Scotland in the form of women's trade unionism and the Women's Liberation Movement (WLM). These often had a common membership, showing that class and feminist politics were not exclusive. As with other countries, this new women's movement saw itself as part of the left, but also recognised that self-organisation was necessary due to misogyny across political parties.

The WLM was not homogenous and contained different groupings. It rapidly expanded the focus of feminist theory and activism to include violence against women, relations in the private sphere, and male-dominated culture. From equal pay to maternity leave, the WLM fought for a new space for women in Scotland, Britain and beyond. Rape Crisis, Women's Aid and Zero Tolerance, feminist groups which continue to support women today, were established in this period.

Women's workplace militancy was also prominent in this period. With women entering the workforce in larger numbers there were attempts by American firms, such as Lee Jeans and Caterpillar, to move beyond the male dominated highly unionised heavy industry in Scotland and use cheap women's un-unionised labour in factories. Yet when these firms tried to shut down in the 1980s it sparked a militant response, with workers locking out managers and organising sit-ins lasting for months. These were huge efforts involving hundreds of workers, almost all women. It is interesting that, despite the press and public support they received at the time, these events are almost forgotten in our history whereas the Upper Clyde Shipbuilders' work-in remains iconic, marked on the contemporary Scottish psyche.

Neoliberalism caused a relative decline in organised and confident oppositional politics, including the women's liberation movement. But in Scotland feminism arguably fared better than elsewhere in Britain, with an effective organisation of women in the run-up to the devolution settlement. Constitutional change provided a catalyst for activists who focused on the issue as a chance to change women's place in Scottish political life. The women's committee of the Scottish Trade Unions Council proposed that there should be gender parity in the new Scottish parliament, kick-starting a programme for women's representation known as the 50:50 campaign.

|| CHALLENGES TODAY ||

Devolution has been termed a "gender revolution", as 37.2 percent of the new MSPs were women. For some this symbolised democratic renewal in Scotland. Yet while this was a great success for feminist organising, achieving levels of representation still unimaginable in Westminster, we should also recognise the limits to this settlement. Little has been done to build on this early progress. Having women in parliament is only one small aspect of women's liberation, and even these small gains can't be sustained without concerted effort by feminists. Numbers of women MSPs are falling; and at the local level they never increased in the first place.

The early years of devolution did bring some small changes for women beyond representation, particularly in a gendered model for tackling domestic violence. Extra parliamentary pressure was effective in enacting progressive legislative change, notably in the case with anti-Section 28 campaigning. This regressive piece of legislation outlawed the "promotion" of homosexuality in schools, effectively banning discussions of and education around LGBT people and relationships. LGBT groups and feminists ran a successful campaign so that the repeal of section 28 (actually section 2A of the relevant Scottish legislation) was one of the first acts of the new parliament.

But devolution never fully realised the potential for change. And at a deeper level, women's liberation across the UK has been regressing over the past 30 years as neoliberalism has become more and more entrenched. Many of the benefits, protections and working rights fought for by women have been taken away; independence can be an opportunity not just to reclaim these but to go beyond that in re-imagining a feminist economy.

The past five years or so has seen something of a resurgence in feminist thought among young women. Disillusioned by the post-feminist, equality-has-been-achieved myth pushed hard in the 1990s, young women have reacted to the real life inequality they experience, and anti-austerity campaigns have reinforced a rise in feminist thought. Young women are blogging, debating and promoting feminist ideas.

It is important not to overstate this resurgence: it is focused largely around elite universities and tends to side-line issues of work or class. But we need this energy in the independence campaign. A feminist independence needs more than free childcare and a vague promise of a more just and equal society, it needs a movement for women's liberation.

WAR AND WOMEN

|| INTRODUCTION ||

In the referendum debate, both official sides agree that Scotland needs strong and powerful armed forces, but disagree on the military impact of independence. For Labour and Conservative unionists, breaking up Britain exposes Scotland (and the world) to massive insecurity. "For the second [largest] military power in the West to shatter…would be cataclysmic," remarked Labour's ex-NATO general secretary Lord George Robertson. "The forces of darkness would simply love it". Albeit in overly excited language, Robertson typifies the mainstream view that Britain's military protects us from "threats", be they Russian, Chinese, or terrorist. Unionists also stress the economic impact of losing military influence. Ex-Tory defence secretary Philip Hammond told Scots to expect serious losses in military jobs like shipbuilding, neglecting to mention over 1,500 job losses at BAE Systems yards in the last 9 months.

Whereas unionist politics is overtly militaristic, there are progressive elements to Yes Scotland's position, particularly on nuclear weapons. Removing Trident from the Clyde presents a huge opportunity for Scotland to take a lead in the world peace movement. However, this important topic can hide strategic similarities between the official Yes side and Better Together. The SNP's reversal of their anti-NATO stance struck a blow against the peace movement, and leading nationalists have sought to reassure American and European leaders that Scotland is a "responsible ally". The SNP's small but influential militarist wing believe Scotland needs a large military after independence.

As feminists we reject the No campaign's narrative: weapons do not keep us safe and military spending is a weak way to guarantee jobs. Most of all, we reject the cross-party consensus at Westminster that Britain needs a nuclear weapons system. High levels of military spending and aggressively interventionist foreign policies do not keep citizens safe, and in fact have an adversely gendered effect, replicating and reproducing inequality between men and women. After independence, Scotland can afford to reduce military spending without compromising security. It can re-invest this money in socially useful jobs, reducing the need for austerity or tax rises. The greatest threat women face is not from rogue states, but rather the threat in their own homes, workplaces and social circles from (plus other threats) domestic and sexual violence. Women in Scotland, the UK and internationally suffer the most from war and conflict, even as Western powers insist they use military power for women's benefit. We wish to demonstrate that reducing Britain's armed forces would, in fact, benefit women internationally as well as domestically.

|| ECONOMIC ISSUES ||

Military jobs have been shamelessly used throughout the referendum debate to manipulate public opinion. Better Together leaders play on understandable fears about employment in the defence sector. But while cutting spending on munitions will lead to some job losses, Scotland would create more jobs by re-investing the money anywhere else. Military spending is among the least efficient way to create jobs. One US study found that $1 billion spending would create 11,200 jobs. By contrast, the same outlay would create 16,800 clean energy jobs, 17,200 health care jobs, or 26,700 education jobs. Re-training workers and re-directing spending can create a secure and sustainable future.

Debates over Trident nuclear missiles typify unionist propaganda. According to Jim Murphy, Labour's Shadow International Development Secretary, independence "would be a fatal blow to Faslane and thousands of jobs throughout the west of Scotland." What Murphy won't mention is that diverting Trident spending could create far more useful civilian jobs. In a report commissioned by Scottish CND and the Scottish Trades Union Congress, the findings show that Scotland will be significantly worse off if Trident is continued, and that investment into Trident actually costs the economy jobs overall.

If nuclear weapons are really a job creation scheme, they are staggeringly ineffective in cost terms; but in reality they are Britain's means of holding rival powers to ransom.

There is no justifiable case for maintaining nuclear weapons on the Clyde, nor any other part of the globe. Even Tony Blair admits there is no military or national security threat that warrants the renewal or replacement of Trident, at what he calls "huge" expense. Blair concedes that Britain only keeps the nukes because removing them would be "too big a downgrading of our status as a nation". Trident embodies Britain's skewed, militaristic public priorities. Despite its reduced status as an American vassal state, the UK is one of the highest global military spenders. After France, China and the USA, no country spends more on the military. Our spending is double South Korea's, even though they have Kim Jong-Un as a near neighbour.

Where Britain prioritises imperial power over the social and economic wellbeing of its citizens, it has a clear gendered impact on society. Tory and Labour leaders at Westminster are unanimous in spending up to £130 billion on Trident replacement. At the same time, they agree that austerity is necessary to safeguard the economy. Report after report has demonstrated that these cuts impact most severely on women. The Fawcett Society even filed papers with the High Court seeking a judicial review of the austerity package, such was the severity of austerity's impact on gender equality. Cuts to public services and social security provision in particular discriminate against women. Jobs in military industries, by contrast, are highly gender-segregated, and their importance in the economy tends to enhance gendered inequalities.

Consequently, aside from the ethics of investing in arms, there is a key issue of opportunity cost. Every pound we commit to the military could be invested elsewhere, creating more, better, safer jobs. Moreover, almost any alternative to military spending would be more progressive in gender terms. While we understand the fears attached to military jobs, it's important to confront the myths, and to highlight the inefficiency as well as the destructiveness of these commitments.

| | SECURING SOCIETY | |

With these economic arguments in mind, a feminist analysis can highlight some of the myths in mainstream accounts of "security". The dominant view says that military spending protects citizens from internal and external threats, and thus spending on arms often goes by the name "defence". Much of this spending is justified by the need to secure Britain from terrorist threats. But even in America, it has been shown that more people are crushed to death by falling furniture or televisions every year than are murdered by terrorists. In the UK, road traffic accidents have caused more deaths in the last decade than terror attacks. By contrast, two British women a week die at the hands of a current or former partner, and one incident of domestic violence is reported every minute.

So what does security really mean? If we take the term seriously, it means living free from anxiety and fear of violence. As shown in chapter 4, women in Britain live in continual insecurity, and they would benefit most from a genuinely "secure" and safe society. But while Britain dedicates billions to confront what Robertson called "the forces of darkness", it does very little to help women who face genuine threats to their safety.

The reality is that domestic and sexual violence are the biggest threats to physical and mental wellbeing. And since austerity began, 40 percent of charities and groups giving support to these victims have lost staff, and 28 percent have lost funding, according to figures from the University of Worcester. While Scotland has done a better job of preserving funding, it's likely that such services could face cuts if austerity continues. Once again, the question of priorities arises. A nation that took security seriously would not waste billions fighting phantom enemies while closing rape crisis centres.

Militarised cultures are intrinsically unsafe for women. One report for the Equal Opportunities Commission showed that a staggering 99 percent of British military women had been exposed to sexual harassment, and 67 percent had suffered directly. The reports also showed only half of reported cases were dealt with effectively. These reflect longstanding trends. A 2003 report found that eight out of ten women in the US armed forces were harassed and a third suffered rape. Research by military historian Professor Madeline Morris has found that societies that undergo war experience more sexual violence even in peacetime. These accounts and statistics reflect the fact that militarism makes life unsafe for women. National chauvinism and gender chauvinism are interrelated; and the practices of sexual humiliation in armed forces have knock-on impacts on society. The redirection of society's resources to better purposes can help create safer communities for women and men alike.

|| INTERNATIONAL ||

One recent trend is to legitimise Western militarism in the language of liberal feminism. In the battle for public support for both the 2003 Iraq war and in Afghanistan, establishment politicians co-opted the rhetoric of "emancipating women". The lurid tortures and abuses of Afghan women by the Taliban, or of Iraqi women by Saddam Hussein lent credence to these views. The answer, for these liberal humanitarians, was to carpet bomb the oppressor. Invasions by Western backers would bring new rights and opportunities to oppressed females who were unable to defend themselves.

This mix of jingoism at home and "freeing" women abroad is actually unoriginal. As Kathy Viner observes:

> ...this theft of feminist rhetoric is not new, particularly if its function is national expansion; in fact, it has a startling parallel with another generation of men who similarly cared little for the liberation of women. The Victorian male establishment, which led the great imperialistic ventures of the 19th century, fought bitterly against women's increasingly vocal feminist demands and occasional successes (a handful going to university; new laws permitting married women to own property); but at the same time, across the globe,

they used the language of feminism to acquire the booty of the colonies.

As most genuine feminists predicted, Western military power proved a staggeringly poor response to the needs of non-Western women. At a cost of trillions, the Iraq War has, by some accounts, set women's rights "back by seventy years". Prior to 1991 Gulf War and economic sanctions against Iraq, women played a key role in Iraq's economy and were able to hold high positions in the private and public sector. Women were assisted in this by labour and employment laws that guaranteed equal pay, six months fully paid maternity leave and protection from sexual harassment. It wasn't until the 1991 Gulf War and U.S.-led economic sanctions against the regime that women's rights in Iraq began to deteriorate. One million Iraqi civilians who slowly starved to death, over half of them children, due to the US-led economic sanctions. As Human Rights Watch has pointed out:

> Women and girls were disproportionately affected by the economic consequences of the U.N. sanctions, and lacked access to food, health care, and education. These effects were compounded by changes in the law that restricted women's mobility and access to the formal sector in an effort to ensure jobs to men and appease conservative religious and tribal groups.

Moreover the invasion of 2003 left Iraqi women and girls vulnerable to rapidly increasing desperation. If British and American leaders genuinely aimed to marry cruise missiles to feminist purposes, they met with (at best) limited success. But of course, this was never the intention. In a typically macho and virile fashion, their real aims were to subordinate oil and gas-rich regions in economic, geo-political, and cultural terms. Their engagement with indigenous feminists was cursory at the best of times, and actively hostile for the majority. Overall, at a staggering cost, a decade of occupation in the Muslim world has arguably set the cause of emancipation back generations. Just as military spending does not keep women safe economically, nor socially, war will never be a tool for women's emancipation. By stealing feminist language, Western leaders associated genuine activists with imperial objectives, which has only led support to misogynists and reactionaries. Militarism and feminist internationalism are incompatible.

|| CONCLUSION ||

To conclude, a Yes vote should lead to a reduction in military spending, which will benefit women in Scotland and beyond. Unless we vote Yes, Britain will remain an American subordinate. As a result, the UK will spend billions to preserve this alliance, its arms industry, and its place on the UN Security Council. Such priorities help to institutionalise sexism by diverting resources away from services which alleviate gender inequality, by cutting support for women suffering abuse and by reinforcing the narrative that women need the assistance of external masculine "helpers" to liberate themselves.

As long as the UK's position as a global military power goes unchallenged these militarist priorities will continue to dominate. Independence is the biggest threat to Britain as a global power since decolonisation, and it provides an opportunity for an independent Scotland to have an independent, fair and just foreign policy.

However, we must confront militaristic views within the SNP and the Yes movement. Already we have seen backsliding over withdrawal from NATO, a traditional nationalist commitment. SNP officials want to commit Scotland to equaling existing numbers in the armed forces, at a cost of £2.5 billion a year. Although this would represent huge savings on our current expenditure, and would rid us of Trident, Scotland would retain unnecessary elements of militarism. As we have shown, this can only damage our society, our culture, and our communities. If Scotland wishes to break from UK patterns of sexism, it should aim for a far more serious redirection of military resources to useful purposes.

---4---

STATES OF VIOLENCE

|| INTRODUCTION ||

Violence against women (VAW) is a global epidemic, shaping women's lives across countries and cultures. To overcome these worldwide realities means tackling the global sources of male power.

We cannot offer this critique here; but we can learn from the specific social, cultural and legal elements of VAW in Scotland and Britain. These are crucial barriers to change for women, and the roots connect to other forms of oppression we suffer. Both genders are victims of violence, but living under its threat defines women's everyday lives.

What's the connection to Scottish independence? It's about the space this debate allow us to rethink civil rights. Nation states routinely deny women full citizenship by becoming complicit in violence in the "private" sphere. So as we set up a new state, it's time for honest reflections on our antiquated approach to rights, privacy, and citizenship, as well as our society's "values". With violence forming a decisive barrier to progress, Scottish society has often failed to openly confront a topic which remains shrouded in misogynistic myths.

We argue that independence can open the space for feminists to transform this culture. As noted in the gender chapter of the *Common Weal*:

Women who have experienced domestic abuse, when asked which interventions would be most effective and helpful, list childcare, housing, income support, and education and skills above refuges. Economic inequality restricts choices, reduces access to justice.

Violence reflects men's power over women; but poverty, instability and absence of personal autonomy reinforce this domination. Thus our ideas about pay, conditions and the care economy under neoliberalism (see chapter 6) are part of this argument.

We see independence as a chance to push essential changes onto political agendas. In particular, topics like corroboration, abortion, asylum and immediate positive reforms for women should instruct the referendum. But public debate and education are just as important as policy, and Scottish feminism must recognise this.

|| Persistent Rape Myths ||

Scottish and British cultures are fully complicit in violence against women. A quarter of women experience serious sexual violence by an intimate partner. 1-in-5 will endure abuse by men in their household. On average, current or former male partners kill two women every week, accounting for a third of all female homicide victims. Overall, almost half of British women suffer domestic violence, molestation or stalking.

Some groups face even harsher fates. Research into sexual violence and domestic abuse against trans people is in its infancy, but studies from the USA show that 50% of trans women have experienced sexual assault. A 2010 Scottish study showed that 80% of trans people suffered similar harassment, most commonly transphobic abuse.

Yet our politics, society, and culture belittles these facts, and the realities they uncover. VAW is routinely denied, ridiculed or overlooked: the rape conviction rate in Scotland is just 7 percent, and that's before considering unreported cases, which are the majority. Tragically, most rapists will never face justice. Commentators and politicians wouldn't accept these statistics for any other crime, violent or otherwise. Rapists act with impunity because women face systematic silencing; even mainstream circles tolerate, condone and arguably encourage it. This acceptance runs through Scottish society from the casual, oh-so-boundary-pushing rape joke (a peculiar "daring" which reinforces standard stereotypes), to outright dismissals of victims as liars.

Given this bigoted legacy, we must problematise our assumptions about family, justice and policy before opinions change. An astounding 27 percent of Scottish people believe that a woman bears partial responsibility for rape if she wears revealing clothing, 29 percent say woman invite it by flirting, and 15 percent think attacks are a women's fault if she's had several sexual partners. All these attitudes confuse rape with sex. But rape, like all VAW, is about domination and control, not sex. No man "needs" to rape; it involves conscious and violent choices. Likewise, women never contribute to or invite violence against them, and rape is horrifying and painful, to a life-changing extent.

Denying that violence is violence helps to silence victims. Many cases aren't given the status of "real rape", which shows the full depths of our cultural misogyny. George Galloway's insistence that "you don't have to ask before every insertion" (yes, you do) reflects pervasive, outdated stereotypes. So, just to be clear: attacking a sleeping woman is rape. If alcohol or drugs prevent knowing consent, it is still rape. If you're married, it is rape. Wherever a woman cannot or will not knowledgeably and enthusiastically consent is rape.

Violent men often target vulnerable women, those with mental health problems, those under the influence of drink or drugs, or those facing isolation. They know rape culture will do the work of denial for them afterwards. The woman is crazy or she can't remember everything that happened, so memories of rape no longer count.

Victims are often accused of lying. Women tell tales habitually, they say, because they are fickle and untrustworthy creatures. They lie for revenge, to seek attention, or out of regret. Never mind that studies show crimes involving violence against women have miniscule levels of false reporting, and that admitting to suffering such violence involves ritual humiliation.

In any case, the system by default assumes women fib, unless there's an Asian or black culprit and a white victim. It assumes victims are liars, despite huge evidence that our societies heave under the weight of men who rape and go free.

So women face a catch 22 condition. We must live under constant suspicion of lying but also on constant lookout for violence. The best advice we're offered is "protecting" ourselves by staying sober, dressing conservatively and only walking in safe places (there are none). When we inevitably flout these rules, we're blamed for any attack.

And this highlights another common rape myth, that attackers are sadistic strangers with knives jumping out the bushes or breaking into your house. In reality, current or former partners commit most attacks, and many other culprits are close acquaintances. Most women knew and trusted their rapists: homes, not night clubs, are the most dangerous places for women. We need to accept that most rapists are normal men, "nice" guys, friends and family members. Teaching women to avoid rape won't work; we should instead teach men not to rape.

In recent years, a new discourse of denial has emerged. Instead of simply ignoring VAW, this strategy confuses the problem by saying men and women suffer in similar proportions. Therefore, the argument goes, tackling violence *per se*, rather than male chauvinism, is the real challenge.

Clearly men can be victims of abuse, and women can be perpetrators. Attacks on men have no less impact, and deserve the same prevention, protection and support. But in truth, men commit 95 percent of sexual assaults on partners. In cases of domestic violence, i.e. on-going violence as opposed to one-off incidents, women are 89 percent of victims. Besides, the men at highest risk are in same-sex relationships, and thus the attackers are men. Additionally, a detailed examination of violence by women shows many cases were reactions to violence by men. Nonetheless, female offenders face arrest three times more commonly.

By definition, VAW is "any act of gender-based violence that results in, or is likely to result in, physical, sexual or mental harm or suffering to women, including threats of such acts, coercion or arbitrary deprivation of liberty, whether occurring in public or in private life." Rape has been examined here, but all anti-women violence involves similar patterns of silencing and dismissal. Rape, sexual harassment, and femicide are all methods of controlling women and preserving oppression.

|| CORROBORATION AND JUSTICE ||

Independence should involve more than simple constitutional tinkering. It can help us challenge existing barriers in the legal system which prevents full justice. The referendum should also prompt a public debate that goes beyond changing laws and borders. While pushing through legislation can bring immediate benefits for women, a broader conversation can deepen change, reforming attitudes which act as barriers to justice and citizenship.

Scots law currently insists that every piece of a criminal charge must be "corroborated". That means every legal part of a case needs two forms of evidence. So, rape cases might need two forms of evidence that penetration took place, two for non-consent, and two showing criminal intent and responsibility.

Of course, VAW is rarely committed before witnesses. And these cases can involve little or no physical injuries that look blindingly obvious to jurors.

Violence against women is often routinised and thus easily dismissed. It could involve a man penetrating a woman as she sleeps at a party, or a husband continuing to have sex with his wife after she wants to stop. Sometimes it's a boyfriend telling his girlfriend that she is stupid and worthless so she should leave the decisions up to him. All these things can destroy women's lives.

Scotland's legal system imposes extra burdens on top of routine disbelief and contempt. Getting women's voices heard in court involves huge, unnecessary barriers.

Only Scotland has this narrow demand for corroboration; even the international criminal courts has nothing similar. Corroboration was progressive centuries ago, before impartial trials, where the word of one feudal lord was enough to condemn someone. But tradition alone doesn't justify anything, otherwise we'd own slaves and women wouldn't vote. Culture is always fluid, and Scottish independence should appeal to our best traditions, not our worst.

Some progressives insist that corroboration protects ordinary people. Without it, anyone protesting can face arrest on false charges, based solely on one police officer's authority, they insist. Or else, poor kids will suffer greater harassment, as police won't need anyone else's word to justify their actions. But one reason officers patrol in twos is to support each other's word in trials. When these cases arise, police simply cover each other, and corroboration offers no protection.

We can't put men's fears before women's realities. Other protections against miscarriages of justice are more effective without compromising attempts to curb rape and violence against women.

However, we must remember that corroboration is not the main cause of low conviction rates. England and Wales now have similarly abject statistics without it. Removing corroboration will only result in a relatively small increase in the number of reported rapes and other forms of violence against women going forward to trial. The true problem is that we live in a society where women are systematically disbelieved.

|| Asylum and Violence Against Women ||

We believe in an open and welcoming Scotland, and thus we oppose immigration borders. But it's not progressive to get so fixated on future ideals that we allow reactionaries to set the agenda in practice. Thus, we want to argue for some specific ideas around asylum, and immigration, policy.

The SNP and the independence campaign are more rhetorically liberal on asylum than Westminster politicians. However, there's little detail on policies for women so far, beyond promises to end detention of pregnant women. While we'll prioritise gender, we also recognise asylum seekers' right to work as a fundamental human right for everyone.

Women may seek asylum for a broad range of issues, many of which men also face. However, persecution is often a gendered experience, and the UK asylum system overlooks and neglects these cases because they fall outside the stereotype of male persecution.

Women claiming asylum on these grounds suffer the same silencing and intimidation as all women. But they do so with the added stress and particular difficulties related to language, or cultural norms such as speaking about such problems in front of men. Even the little respect and sensitivity granted to women in broader society doesn't extend to women seeking refuge.

Some of these topics are not specific to asylum seekers, but instead reflect society-wide racism and discrimination. But women fleeing persecution face these problems on a radical scale. Certain groups of women can endure particular forms of dismissal: LGBTQ women have been asked to "prove" their lesbian, gay, bisexual, trans or queer status. Clearly, that task is fraught with difficulties.

Asylum rights must form part of the public discussion around violence against women and independence. We should demand simple dignity: end the humiliating questioning, end demands for proof of being LGBTQ, and give asylum-claiming women the same respect as others.

|| THE RIGHT TO CHOOSE ||

The independence referendum gives Scotland a choice: to be independent but also to choose our values. This topic should stretch beyond nationhood, to cover control over our bodies. To deny abortion rights is to commit institutional violence against women, giving states power over our bodies without consent.

Britain's abortion system surrounds us with legislative misogyny backed up by cultural bigotry. Women must get permission from two doctors, who agree that continuing a pregnancy would worsen their mental or physical health, or that of their existing children, more than termination. This may often be a formality, but it lengthens the process, wastes NHS time, and causes unnecessary fear and anxiety for women.

These rules give doctors ownership and control of our bodies. And seizing abortion from women's hands has damaging outcomes. Around 1-in-10 doctors oppose abortion, and although they must refer women immediately to another practitioner, some use the opportunity to delay or obstruct the decision.

Yet a discourse of secrecy and shame still surrounds abortion. Even clear pro-choice supporters fall into this rhetoric: so in a speech in 2008 defending the right to abortion Diane Abbott said "every abortion is a tragedy". This concedes that abortion is wrong, forgivable only when circumstances allow no alternative. In reality, women have abortions and don't feel guilt, because they haven't done anything bad. Of course, some women feel loss or shame and they need support. But we shouldn't assume, for convenience's sake, the tragic nature of abortion; it's a right and a free choice.

Abbott also tacitly belittles non-tragic abortions, implying their link to bad lifestyles. There's a persistent implication that women who have several abortions are wanton hussies. By asking for an abortion, a woman opens herself to bigoted character judgement. First, she must confront the system's assessments, and second, she faces society's "slutshaming". Whether a woman gets pregnant through rape or through anonymous sex, whether the abortion is her first or fifth, should be irrelevant.

Young people face heightened moral judgements. Since they don't have some magic way to prevent pregnancy, some young people will get pregnant and some will choose to end that pregnancy. Teenage abortions are rising at roughly the same rate as rates of teenage births are falling. Moral panics about abortion-happy teens become proxies for broader anxieties about young women taking their own decisions.

We believe that anyone should have abortion rights on demand, regardless of the circumstances; getting pregnant shouldn't be criminalised. But in addition, there is mounting evidence that loosening the grip of stigma and prejudice reduces abortions and – in particular – late-term abortions. This is probably because improved access to services (contraception and abortion) and more progressive societal attitudes allow people to seek help and advice earlier. Canada, for example, is one of few countries to permit abortion on demand, yet has low abortion levels and fewer late term abortions than more restrictive nations. The same trend applies worldwide.

So let's be clear: nobody should judge the morality of pregnancy because there aren't bad reasons for abortion. An independent Scotland which challenges women's oppression must include the right to abortion on demand.

|| BEYOND THE LAW ||

In all of the above discussions on legal reform one thing comes out strongly: that it is necessary but far away from sufficient. This is not a new point to make. Having good laws cannot overrule the way in which these laws play out on the ground in a society based on misogyny. We need to change the way we talk about violence against women so that rape is no longer the only crime where the victim and not the defendant is on trial. And above all so that violence does not happen in the first place.

Scotland has taken some steps in this direction due to the consistent work of feminist organisations. The importance of education is officially recognised by the Scottish Executive and initiatives by Zero Tolerance have designed interventions across schools and, importantly early years work with parents and in nurseries for children under the age of five. Important because we know that world views, including how children view gender, are often formed before they reach school age. This should be more than initiatives however; it should be a compulsory aspect woven through the entire curriculum and set up of our childcare and education systems. If we want our children to grow up with inquisitive and innovative minds this is an ideal way to make them think critically about the world around them. However, education that focuses on formal institutions will always fall short as it is constantly fighting against wider societal attitudes. While every drop of education may be a step forward for future generations we need to go beyond this.

Feminist organisations today have an unprecedented relationship with the Scottish Executive. This is positive as groups have been able to have an impact on policy. However, this has come at the expense of real public engagement-now limited to media campaigns and education initiatives. Feminists need to link policy work with public engagement and participation-they need to become part of a movement again. This may be harder work in the short-term, as it may involve engaging with backwards sections of the public. However, real changes in violence against women will not come from the state but from a change in public will. The patriarchal state will concede a certain amount to feminist arguments in order to maintain its legitimacy but there is a limit that we are fast approaching to how much they will really change society.

We also need to be aware that the linking of violence against women to a law and order agenda has profoundly alienating impacts for many women, particularly those in marginalised communities. The current focus on policing, including community policing, legitimises the force of the state against ordinary people. When your experience of police is them harassing you, pinning you to the ground, or multiple gratuitous stop and searches, having increased police and a crackdown on "crime" is unlikely to help you feel safer. And the impact on violence in the home is negligible. This is not to say that we oppose in any way women who use the police and courts, it is the only way we have of getting some form of justice. But it is important to remember that these are part of a patriarchal state.

This links to out arguments around radical participatory democracy-violence against women needs to be part of a full democratic debate within society. Much has been made of Scotland's supposed high level of civil society engagement since the devolution campaign. We must be clear-this "civil society" is an interest group that promotes professional and middle class concerns and solutions. We need a radical civil society of the Scottish population that does not just consult marginalised groups-working class women, LGBTQ women, BME women, disabled women-but has them at the heart and leading the debate. Only in this way can we turn the tide on violence against women.

5

CULTURE AND DESPAIR

|| INTRODUCTION ||

A recent report by Rashida Manjoo, the UN rapporteur on violence against women, found that Britain's "boys' club sexist culture" was worse than any country she had visited including India, Algeria and Italy. Shortly afterwards, former Conservative health minister Edwina Currie dismissed the comments: "Most of the women I know like living here and enjoy being in a diverse and interesting society," she remarked.

This illuminates two features of British culture: it remains brashly and toxically sexist; and it marches on in blind denial. They tell us sexism happens elsewhere, in "uncivilised" places, by brutish men against submissive women. "At least we're not Saudi Arabia," we're told, a misogynistic take on the global race to the bottom.

As with violence, our sexist culture precludes the participation and full citizenship of women. And again, separating the particular situation of Scotland and Britain from broader gender hierarchies poses problems. But sexist stereotypes and misogyny takes different forms in different societies. Can we make culture – women's everyday culture as opposed to nationalist stereotypes – part of the debate on independence? Of course, this is a two way argument: culture affects and can affect our economy and politics. What can we learn from the most progressive gender parts of our culture, our feminist tradition?

|| BRITISH TRADITIONS ||

Dominic Mohan, ex-editor of *The Sun*, recently called Page 3 an "innocuous British tradition". In this view, "real" sexism is long past: if a newspaper wants to print boobs, and men like staring at them, it's just "harmless fun". The real battles have already been won: after all, this is no longer the 1950s, women are free to choose.

Yet we are thrust into a rigid gender binary from the moment we're born, declared male or female and by extension a girl or boy. This guides our lives, our opportunities and others' expectations of us. Being a man or a woman – and you must always be one or the other – controls our whole existence. In Britain today, we are still taught that men are strong, rational and assertive while women are weak, emotional and passive. And while stereotypes damage everyone, they exist in a strict hierarchy which values "male" virtues over "female" ones.

Capitalist patriarchy has reformed over the past few decades. But we need to be clear that change does not nullify sexism. Patriarchy no longer excludes female CEOs, lawyers or bankers. In fact, although most women can never reach these levels, contemporary ideology values the few women who gain admittance to the upper echelons. Indeed, it needs them; because today, if you can't achieve the same as men around you, it's your own fault, not sexism's fault. Rather than confront barriers, we are urged to be more confident, learn the game better, assert ourselves more.

Today's patriarchy is dangerous because it is subtler and does not always rely on obviously unjust laws to control what women do. Instead it creates an illusion of choice, so we do not question or even see our constrictions. An exploration of sexist stereotyping and misogynist practices can illustrate the reality for women in their everyday lives. We shall start by looking at how Britain's sexist culture works through a broader culture of privatisation and our truncated democracy, nurturing the so-called boys' club.

|| SEXISM AND PRIVATISATION ||

Britain, and thus Scotland, follows worldwide norms in its habitual sexism. Sexist stereotypes reflect the complex history of Western political and economic structures. It would be impossible here to provide a comprehensive overview of how sexism works through UK institutions. However, it is important to consider some elements of a peculiarly chauvinist British public sphere.

Research shows that societies with well-funded public sectors are more gender-equal. This particularly applies to non-military spending. While Britain reflects global trends of privatisation, cheap labour and tax breaks, it also actively enforces and promotes free market restructuring. Forty-percent of the total value of all privatisations in the Western world between 1980 and 1996 happened in the UK. And as discussed in chapter 3, British military spending is disproportionately high. While the Scottish government champions social democratic values, and often mitigates select Westminster policies, Holyrood has also enforced market orthodoxy (see chapter 6).

In comparison with the Nordic model, researcher Dominic Hynde notes that Scottish public space is "firmly British", i.e. homogenous and highly commercial. A 2013 UNICEF study argued that Britain's pro-market society, compared to Spain and Sweden, clearly damages the well-being of children and fosters sexualised views of women. While privatisation and commercialism don't directly cause sexism, they do accelerate it.

Britain's political culture also influences sexism's appearance. The first-past-the-post system favours white, successful men, by making the candidate's "capability", not the party's politics, the issue. And in sexist societies, individual men are usually seen as more capable than individual women, creating a self-reinforcing cycle.

Even by the standards of parliamentary democracies in crisis, Britain's is particularly staid (we will look beyond this in chapter 7). This conformity goes beyond the formal sphere to shape our daily political culture, and despite cosmetic changes at Holyrood, Scotland is no exception. We need a new approach to democracy.

|| CULTURES OF HARM? ||

Given that many deny sexism's existence, or dismiss it as harmless, we should recall some general points about women's subordination. Stereotyping surrounds us and it is never harmless: it is part of a spectrum that sometimes ends with rape or other forms of violence.

From day one, even before we can talk, babies get different treatment based on their gender: beautiful little girl, big strong boy. Toy stereotyping – pink dolls for girls and blue action figures for boys – is widely commented on, and justifiably so. How can children choose their future when their present is narrowed down for them?

In education, we still speak of "boys'" and "girls'" subjects; there are still also men's jobs and women's jobs. This is not only about parents: true gender-neutral child rearing is impossible as we cannot remove ourselves or our children from society's influence. Nor is this just about children. Here we would like to explore a couple of the ways in which sexism in our society works to control women and constrict our lives.

|| The Beauty Industry ||

Our culture is obsessed with female beauty. As women we are judged on our appearance far more than our abilities or achievements: beauty is held as our ultimate goal. And the idea of beauty is not about stupid, vain or neurotic women with nothing better to do; it's about how capitalism enforces social control.

Often, the ideology of beauty masquerades as a celebration of women. Many insist it's natural for women, or even people, to want to please others and look good. But the beauty industry doesn't aim to make women feel good; its real success lies in making women feel bad. We must continually judge ourselves against ideal, unachievable images. Women spend hours plucking, shaving, putting on make-up and choosing clothes. The beauty industry is big business – worth hundreds of billions, it is growing fast across the planet. The industry thrives on the doubts and insecurities it fosters in women.

We must insist that women who buy hair extensions, go to tanning salons or get Brazilians are not to blame. Readers of "trashy" magazines aren't the problem either. Capitalism relies on selling dissected parts of our resistance back to us; hence, parts of the industry focus on "natural" beauty or saying women are pretty no matter their size or shape. But this just creates an alternative perfection and an equally false ideology of "nature". This misses the causes of these neuroses in our capitalist society, blaming the individual instead. The effect is denigrating and isolating women who feel guilty for their insecurities.

The beauty industry cannot tackle the problem of body image: without these anxieties, it couldn't exist. It's not enough to say commerce distorts true beauty, because beauty doesn't exist beyond society. Natural or real beauty is a myth: capitalist culture manufactures these obsessions.

The beauty industry's overwhelming conformity makes it virulently racist. Reflecting dominant cultures, beauty is always white, and non-white women are allowed to be beautiful only within the context of racist stereotyping. So women are exotic, dressed in "tribal" outfits or made to appear animalistic. The beauty industry knows this; they promote, exploit, and reinforce it. Currently a common plastic surgery is eye-widening or inserting a fold into the eyelid to make eyes appear more "European" or whiter. Skin-whitening creams are big business, directly linking lighter skin tone to beauty.

While these trends apply worldwide, there remains a very specific British component. British women are among Europe's most anxious when it comes to physical appearance. Such insecurities can take a violent form, and here the UK fares badly again. Anorexia and bulimia are increasing across Europe but Britain consistently has the highest levels, as women desperately try to claw back control of their bodies.

|| SEXUALITY AND SOCIETY ||

Female bodies are everywhere, yet women's voices are nowhere. We are bombarded with images of posed and perfect women, teaching us that our greatest virtue is availability to men. The media promotes the idea that women are now "free" to be sexual, having destroyed the bonds of past repression. But this sexuality controls without empowering.

Again, although the UK is not unique, British culture exaggerates its sharpest features. Lad culture, that generalisation of elitist arrogant public school rugby culture, glories in the sexual harassment and humiliation of women. It creates a new boys' club culture, bullying women into sexualised situations.

There is a spectrum of control of women's bodies and sexualities: commodification of our bodies at one end, rape and violence at the other. On the surface, each page 3, each sexualised image of a woman, appears a harmless bit of fun. But together these dehumanise women, turning people into objects.

Having achieved the sexual subordination of women, society criticises us for it. Having taught women the virtues of self-commodification, it is turned back on us. Women are called sluts, told they are a bad example for others, or they are condemned for using their body to get ahead. There is a particular panic around young women, based on some legitimate problems. They have grown up under far more sexualised consumer pressure than their parents. But in official discourse, genuine concerns give way to moralistic instruction about appropriate dress and actions. And this has a strong class element: middle class pundits are especially vicious when confronted with stereotypes of working class women smoking on their second pregnancy, eating chips and blindly following celebrity trivia.

The focus is always on the behaviour and bodies of women. We need to turn this on its head. Women do not need to cover up or have less sex. Nor do they need to have more. Women should be free to do what they want with their bodies free from all forms of coercion.

|| THE REAL WORLD ONLINE? ||

The internet is changing societies worldwide. The first generation to grow up with the internet are now adults and many spend hours a day online, forming communities and interacting. For many women it shapes their everyday life and it cannot be ignored or wished away. Recently, sexist trolling and the new spaces for online misogyny have created new debates about gender and identity.

It's popular to see the internet as the villain. But the internet does not create sexism: it provides a platform for sexism that already exists. The internet naturally reflects male domination in our social structures. Most blogs are written by men, most forums are aimed at men and most commenters are men. Online advertising and media perpetrate ideologies of gender drawn from elsewhere.

The internet can also be an exclusive space. Only 68 percent of Scottish households, and 57 percent of Glaswegian households, have internet access. Others may officially have access but don't engage in online community. We can also make a reasonable assumption that many in these excluded groups are from already marginalised backgrounds. Difficulties of written expression (more than 20% of Scottish adults are functionally illiterate, rising to 40% in certain areas) can exclude many groups. Also, women have far less time for leisure, including online participation. Nonetheless, young women are more likely to achieve feminist consciousness by reading blogs and online discussions than through formal feminist meetings. The internet helps women to access a community of support; and for some women, such as those with disabilities, it's an inclusive meeting space compared to real world locations. Online activism has its limits: "clicktivism" can satiate radical impulses, as people gain a false sense of purpose by merely retweeting. But it remains a significant tool. Some say the Yes campaign has won the Twitter war; what about a feminist independence?

|| FEMINIST FAILURES: TRANS INCLUSION ||

Although we refer to women throughout this book, we also stress as feminists that gender binaries are social constructions. Many people identify outside of these two groups and feminism must include those oppressed as if they were women.

We would like to mention a particular group of women: that of trans women. Why? Because this particular group of women are too often denied this status. Worse, some of this comes from people who call themselves feminists.

Some feminist transphobia comes from a mistaken belief that the existence of trans people reinforces the idea that gender roles are biological not social. Many trans women may buy into gender stereotypes. Yet this seems to willingly overlook that the majority of cis women – that is women who are not trans – do this too. Also, this is something that is forced on trans women in a different way to cis women. For trans women to gain acceptance, they must adopt social cues that others accept as part of femininity: few cis women face a similar reality.

The problem is that societies impose strict rules of admittance for male and female identity. Nobody is born a woman: we all create ourselves in varying versions of womanhood. But trans people question the nature of both sex and gender, creating radical potential for opening a discussion on cultural constructions.

Being at the sharp point of marginalisation, it is difficult to gather reliable statistics on numbers of trans, agender, or gender-queer people, but some American estimates have ranged from 0.5 to 5 percent of the population. Although Scottish figures have shown much lower figures, this may reflect cultural stereotypes, fear, and (most of all) very limited funding for data collection. Even on conservative estimates, there are probably tens of thousands of Scots who don't fit the gender binary, and we need to include this in our debate on feminism if we are to create an inclusive independence.

|| Masculinities ||

Debates about gender often focus only on women, unintentionally reinforcing the idea that women are gendered, men are simply the norm to be compared against. Yet men and masculinity are constructed, just like women and femininity. We must challenge men and masculinity as default states, turning everyone else into deviant "others".

Men dominate space in society, so we do not argue that women should look at men's problems. And although men also suffer from gender norms, the solution is achieving women's liberation. Too much space in our society is already taken up looking at men. Nonetheless, male behaviour is not natural and can be changed. Feminist men can play an important role here in questioning masculinity and maleness. There is an old feminist saying: feminist men should not take up feminist space, they should make their space more feminist.

|| A New Scotland? ||

How can independence be a tool for changing Scotland's culture? As with other northern European countries, our laws and formal equality have made little progress in challenging ingrained views on men and women. As we undergo a national conversation about the society we want, we must prioritise confronting stereotyping, sexism and transphobia.

Like violence against women, this opening in the normally closed political culture provides a unique chance to educate others. This is not a nationalist argument: Scotland does not have a uniquely progressive outlook on gender. But in 2014 we have a space for dialogue. The Westminster consensus gives no such opportunity.

Other countries provide better examples for opening a debate. India recently changed its laws to recognise a third gender: it is no longer compulsory to be either male or female. Sweden officially instituted a gender neutral pronoun. Any such change should be designed by trans and nonbinary people in order that it does not inadvertently reinforce their third class status. "Third gender" status can be used, for example, to deny that trans people are their gender: so trans women are not women but different. The German law of last year, which gives a third gender option, was criticised by intersex groups because doctors will make the decision not parents. It may result in more pressure for surgery which has been condemned by the UN as damaging. Moreover, third gender laws substitute a three way divide for a binary. But they can offer campaigning points to open a broader conversation on gender.

There is nothing natural about gender stereotyping, and this can be part of the debate around independence. Can we also have independence from restrictive and dangerous gender norms? Should children be referred to by gender in nurseries and schools? Should they be divided by gender in sports? Should we continue with advertising that uses the bodies of women? Should an abstract and individualised right to freedom of expression be allowed to perpetuate harm through sexist jokes?

Legal change is not always the answer. But we need to make these questions part of the debate, about the values shaping Scotland's independence. We need to take stories of everyday sexism, and everyday gender assumptions, and subject them to political change. We cannot remove ourselves from prevalent social attitudes. We can only fight to change them.

6

BRITAIN COUNTS US OUT

|| INTRODUCION ||

Economics has dominated the independence debate. This is partly because, unlike many national movements, Scots aren't rebelling against colonial oppressors: Scots fully shared the Empire's spoils with England. Statehood therefore has no predefined ethical purpose, and the case for independence must stress its pragmatic ends. While national identity matters for some voters, existential Scottishness doesn't explain voting patterns either. Austerity and a failing economy dominate all world debates, and in reality this referendum is no different. Inequality has thus become the crucial dividing line in independence support, reflecting broader world trends but also discontent at Westminster's many-sided legitimacy crisis, from elite privilege to reckless cuts.

Better Together, despite their denials, aim to convince Scots that surviving alone is impossible, and that changing the status quo is too risky. They rarely need to prove this argument: it's often enough to forewarn of lurking terrors and impose a climate of fear.

By contrast, Yes Scotland alternates between pitching Nordic-inspired buzzwords of equality and fairness while also eulogising our (past and present) enterprising individualism. They foster illusions in Scotland's natural communitarian instinct, while staying silent on class divisions.

Both SNP-guided Yes Scotland officials and Better Together share an emphasis on economic continuity, guided by pro-business assumptions. Transferring power from London to Edinburgh won't automatically change this, and the debate needs clear perspectives on where wealth and power lie in Scotland, so we can tell voters what we want independence for.

Nationalists rightly insist that Scotland is a wealthy capitalist nation. If Scotland became independent now it would be the sixth richest OECD country based on gross domestic profit (GDP) per head, substantially ahead of the UK at number 15. If this is surprising, given the visible poverty in Scotland, it shows the need to dig beneath official GDP statistics when assessing a country's prosperity. Proclaiming Scotland's riches is not enough; we need to know who owns and controls resources. Elite Scots own 260 times more wealth than the bottom 10 percent, and merely changing a Union Jack to a Saltire won't improve these statistics.

While the radical Yes movement has drawn attention to divisions of wealth and income, even this strand has left gender inequality under-theorised. The gender-blind approach risks us losing touch with women, who suffer most from the Westminster consensus. Of course, the White Paper makes some gestures towards "women's issues", but these are easily, and perhaps rightly, dismissed as tokenism.

Across Scotland, women are as concerned about the economy as men, but no side of the debate has done enough thinking on the topic. Class is at the heart of independence; but gender is at the heart of class.

|| AUSTERITY AND GENDER ||

Although the devolved parliament mitigates certain cuts, Scots live in austerity Britain, against a backdrop of soaring inequality. While cuts hit communities across the UK, the wealth of the 1000 richest people rose by 15.4 percent last year to £518.975 billion. Meanwhile the number of children in Scotland living in poverty rose by 30,000 over the last year.

And austerity doesn't just take from working people: it takes specifically from women. House of Commons Library research shows that from the 2010 budget onwards, 74.8 percent of fiscal budget cuts have fallen chiefly on women. Women make up two-thirds of public sector employees and are more likely to use public services, meaning we're hit hardest by cuts. Women's unemployment is at a 25 year high and increasingly investment focuses on male-dominated areas (60% of new private sector jobs since 2010 have gone to men). For women, part-time work is growing at the expense of full-time, suggesting underemployment disguised beneath the official job statistics.

Clearly, employment is not a zero-sum game: employment for men does not mean unemployment for women or vice versa; it's possible to create jobs for both genders. However, there's a clear and undeniable trend whereby Britain's investment freeze hits women harder.

So far Westminster has only imposed 25 percent of their planned cuts. The damage is already vast, before most austerity measures, including a planned extra £10 billion cut from welfare spending, have even arrived. When this happens, if current trends continue, women's relative living standards will fall, probably by a large measure.

As states slash benefits, women pick up most of the burden in caring for children, the sick and, increasingly in an aging population, the elderly. It is women who make sure household budgets balance, and who suffer most from the psychologically-draining task of putting food on the table. Often it's mothers who must turn to food banks first.

Some measures, like child benefit cuts for higher tax rate payers, have more subtle reactionary implications. At first, since they hit those already on fair incomes, they seem innocent: but in reality, in many households, a women's only independent income is child benefit. Since money is a key source of power and control in relationships, removing women's autonomous income makes it likelier some will stay with abusive men.

Currently, Westminster controls welfare in Scotland, and since all main parties promise more austerity, then regardless of 2015's election result, severe cuts will further erode women's status. Their wealth, health, happiness, comfort, security and safety are on the chopping block. The UK model is indefensible for women, and any opportunity to break from it is welcome.

| | Devolution Disillusionments | |

Against the background of Westminster's failures, Scotland's political class, especially the SNP, can present themselves as competent social democrats. Since devolution, both main parties talk positively about social justice (although their practice is questionable), in contrast to Westminster's free market authoritarianism. While UK politics pivots on the New Labour-Tory axis, Scotland's centre-ground is far less draconian and far more open to public solutions.

Holyrood's claim to do social democracy better partly rests on its supposed moves towards gender equality. And, true, there have been undeniable successes. On top of increasing women's representation, Holyrood enshrined equality as one of its four founding principles; and, relative to Westminster, Scottish leaders are far more serious about tackling violence against women as a gendered problem. Populist measures like free prescriptions also disproportionately benefit women.

So has devolution heralded a new age of gender equality in Scotland? Some commentators have certainly thought so. "Nothing, but nothing, will now cause this issue [gender equality] to go away," Tom Nairn announced in 1994. "It has become a small-'n' nationalist banner, an emblem of the kind of country and the style of nationalism people really want."

But how can Scotland's political class square all this bluster with a later record of poor progress on the gender pay gap and women's evermore precarious employment?

The truth is while Holyrood freed leaders to spout social democratic buzzwords, they embraced neoliberalism in practice. After devolution, Scottish Labour gave private finance initiatives (PFIs) their unqualified blessing, allowing corporations to rake in unheard-of profits from critical services. Meanwhile, parallel to this, financialisation in Scotland surpassed the rest of the UK, including London. So pro-market governance, with light touch regulation and low-wages, was Scotland's actual direction of policy. Needless to say, such preferences ran counter to the interests of those who voted in good faith for social democracy.

It's easy to forget, as Westminster austerity sets new horizons for cruelty, that gender has been central to the neoliberal system for decades. It is women who use state services, and they suffer greater impacts from privatisation and cuts. The post-Thatcher policy consensus has involved a counter-reformism, in which equality for women is no longer a substantive consideration.

Some might protest that devolution has brought benefits to Scotland. Rightly, they point out that, without it, Scotland would pay for prescriptions, (Scottish) students would face £9,000 fees, and the NHS would be privatised to an even greater degree. We also admit that these Holyrood victories are vital for women's livelihoods, and naturally we support such measures. But only in an era of crumbling hopes and omnipotent fears could anyone embrace these small successes as signs of democracy in good health. We shouldn't exaggerate our few random crumbs from the neoliberal table.

|| NORDIC PARADISES? ||

For parts of the independence campaign, Nordicism is the new common sense. Many insist Scotland can simply jump into this model, having removed the yoke of Britain and London rule. Nor is Nordicism merely a fringe concern: the SNP's White Paper refers more to Norway, Sweden and Denmark each than to Britain. SNP leaders are likely to have cynical motives for this, hoping that voters conflate Nordicism's positive connotations with the vaguer Salmond-Sturgeon agenda for "fairness", which tries to marry Anglo-American tax cutting with Scandinavian welfare spending.

Nordicism also goes beyond narrow party agendas. More substantial programs like the Common Weal aim to resolve the SNP model's contradictions by suggesting properly-financed Nordic-style mixed economies, with higher taxes to fund more government intervention.

But a one-sided version of this approach can also foster illusions. Doubtless, by UK standards, Scandinavia has delayed social democracy's decline, but the past decade has seen rampant privatisation, financial deregulation and cuts to welfare. The far-right has grown at disturbing rates, and last year's riots in south Sweden against police harassment of mainly immigrant youths should dispel easy assumptions about social harmony. Indeed, while the number of women entering high positions is still rising, gender equality across the board has stalled.

There is also a deeper, sociological problem: European welfare states emerged from decades of class struggle, as an uncomfortable and ultimately doomed compromise between workers, farmers, and the ruling class. This was not a tamed capitalism happily handing-down wealth. Socialist agendas cannot base themselves on expectations of government benevolence, even if they can rely on truly well-intentioned politicians, because this ignores the power of global capitalism. We inhabit a world system where the rich of the north depend on exploiting workers at home and super-exploiting the Global South. We cannot escape this by act of will: we need to change where the power lies.

Despite these problems, we should seriously assess attractions of Nordic examples. They show that better models are possible even within capitalist limits, and that neoliberalism, while damaging social solidarity worldwide, has uneven effects. They also prove, contrary to Unionist propaganda, that size isn't a barrier to good policy. We should not slight these achievements: reforms can help transform people's lives. Scandinavian countries regularly top gender equality rankings such as in the World Economic Forum's Global Gender Gap Report. Feminist mobilisation for change combined with strong welfare cultures has resulted in a raft of measures aimed at reducing inequality. Norway, for example, has legislation requiring 40 percent of public and private boards to be women. It was the first country to introduce a Gender Equality (and Anti-Discrimination) Ombud to enforce the Gender Equality Act. Maternity and paternity provisions vary across the region, but all outrank the UK, whose system has been assessed second worst in Europe.

There is no barrier to independent Scotland setting up similar measures. Currently the SNP promise to "consider" quotas in public and private boards, but if these already work in the world's most prosperous nations, why not make them compulsory? There are few excuses. Similarly, an independent Scotland should enforce basic social rights, by extending maternity and paternity leave and expanding the SNP's current childcare proposals.

But even at this basic level, examined in more detail, Scandinavian successes are actually more mixed and contradictory. The gender equality measures already cited tend to focus on levels of economic participation, educational achievement and women in positions of power or promoted positions. Yet when measures such as horizontal segregation – the clustering of men and women in certain occupations – or care-in-the-home are introduced, Scandinavian countries fare far less well. Sometimes their successes even fall below Southern Europe. Scandinavia still positions women in "women's work", and although everyone's jobs are more secure than the UK, women inhabit those with lower pay and security. The burden of care is also still on women, despite the successes of subsidised childcare.

Of course Scotland should aim to match Scandinavian successes, but we must ask ourselves why our ambitions stop at this flawed and declining model. If we want to tear at the roots, we need to think about women's position across the economy, not just at the elite levels. Indeed, merely examining the waged economy is not enough either. Therefore, in the next section, we will consider how Britain's economy divides work between genders today, and this will form the basis of our own proposals.

|| WOMEN'S REALITY TODAY ||

Women and men live different daily realities. The myth that women stay at home and men go to work was never true for most women, and it certainly isn't true today. Yet it is true that men's and women's lives are structured by distinct pressures and controls. We often work in separate areas and socialise in different spaces; and men largely occupy public political space.

We should be under no illusions, our society remains segregated. We have already looked at stereotyping and divisions forced on us by society; here, we want to see how this applies in workforces. To fully appreciate how our economy involves more women while retaining segregation in paid and unpaid work, we must understand how states, including our Scottish government, enforce exposure to market conditions. Creating a different tomorrow starts with understanding today's norms and expectations.

|| WORK IN A SEGREGATED ECONOMY ||

In nearly all developed societies, the number of working women has increased since WWII. Britain and Scotland follow that pattern, with large increases in labour force participation, and in this narrow sense, the gender gap has narrowed or even been eliminated. But in other respects, inequalities have not "dissolved" at all. Yes, more women occupy top jobs, in executive and professional positions; but for most, working means exposure to the UK's chronic low-pay economy. Thus, beneath a media façade of empowered women with successful careers, Britain has one of Northern Europe's biggest gender pay gaps.

In all capitalist economies, men and women occupy different roles and spaces, and these gendered positions are arranged in hierarchical order. Informal gender segregation works in two ways: vertically, in that within particular occupations men occupy promoted positions while women occupy lower grades; and horizontally, i.e. men are clustered in different jobs than women. Traditionally, lower-paid occupations remain overwhelmingly dominated by women (e.g. 82% of workers in "caring, leisure and other services", and 77% of administrative and secretarial workers are women). The 5 "C's"- cleaning, catering, caring, cashiering and clerical work – remain resolutely female, while men are scattered over a wider range of jobs.

Today, women's pay, terms and conditions are deteriorating, with austerity sharpening an already existing trend. In the public sector, austerity has increased pension contributions and also the age at which pensions can be drawn, and under present conditions it is likely to rise further. Young women under the current system won't get a pension until they're physically unable to work longer. This comes on top of a two-year wage freeze meaning that the real income of public sector workers is dropping. In the private sector, particularly for women as they are crowded on the very bottom rung, pay and conditions have started at bad and gone to worse.

|| CARE ECONOMY ||

Women are in a constant juggling act. We do housework, provide emotional support, look after children, look after the sick, do paid work, look after elderly family members and fit this round organising general family life. Women have moved into paid work in ever greater numbers but men have not moved in the opposite direction. Women are still the carers, the cleaners, and the workers. Meanwhile the UK has one of the highest costs of childcare in the world. Women can't afford not to work, but they also cannot currently afford to work.

This is why the White Paper's key "feminist" policy, free childcare at the point of use, has been so welcomed by many women. Many working women experience childcare as a huge burden, and know that their own lives, and their children's, will improve from more quality time and disposable income.

However, in the White Paper this policy is couched in terms of women's labour market participation: the overall message is not about equality but that people (women) are only societally valuable if they do paid work.

The SNP proposal could have gone further: it only covers the equivalent of a primary school day and few people can find a job that wants them only between 9-3 on weekdays. Parents will still be forced to find extra care in order to be part of the paid workforce.

However, to really address the imbalance in men and women's power, in an Independent Scotland, we must move beyond just talking about "childcare", but about the *care economy*. "Women's work" in unpaid care and reproductive roles is absolutely central to our economy, but it's excluded from discussion.

The only acknowledgement of the role women play is in that backhanded exploitation that is "flexible" working. Of course, real flexibility would be a good thing. But flexible working has become a way of making care work ever more the problem of individual women: don't struggle to change our role in society, just get a flexible job and work around it.

| | PATHWAYS FORWARD? | |

As we have shown, the material reality for Scottish women today is the low wage, precarious economy allied to overwhelming care duties. The SNP and Yes Scotland have offered nothing to suggest significant movement on either of these areas. The White Paper promises to end the ugliest Westminster welfare cuts but little in terms of changing how the economy as a whole is biased against women. The word "gender" is mentioned only 16 times and only 6 in relation to shifting the balance of power between men and women (even these limited references are about public and private boardrooms, which changes little for ordinary women).

Their childcare proposals are definitely welcome, but they're not a panacea. If we aim for substantive change, we need to consider how our economy positions women overall: as carers, in low-paid insecure employment. Ultimately, these are problems embedded in the global economic structure. Our fundamental aim must be to build power and legitimacy from below to socialise wealth and power.

The question then is: what can independence offer this vision? By being an independent state, Scotland would have control over its own economic and financial policy; in this sense, political debates will be sharpened, since politicians can no longer attribute failings to Westminster's bias. The progressive discourse around independence also creates momentum for meaningful change. Indeed, it perhaps offers the potential for more than this. By gaining reforms to improve life and build women's confidence, this can catalyse further demands and new possibilities.

We have outlined the limits of the Nordic model in this chapter. However, we stress that we absolutely support those policies where these countries outstrip the current proposals in Scotland, such as legislative quotas for public and private boards. We also fully support investment in welfare, because a strong public sector is important for gender equality. But the true challenge is building women's economic power from below.

Therefore we offer here 6 immediate demands that put women workers before the needs of private capital. These may not be particularly radical in an abstract sense, but they can provide a starting point for an independent women's agenda.

|| A Compulsory Living Wage ||

The very idea that Scotland's minimum wage won't cover minimum basic needs is absurd. The White Paper promises to raise the legal minimum in line with inflation, but this merely preserves poverty at its current level. An independent Scotland should set its minimum wage at the level of a living wage, and let this rise with inflation.

This could allow low paid workers, who are mainly women, a measure of decency. However, if this is run as a campaign it could also show how poverty wages are not a necessity that women must accept. Rather women can fight to improve their own interests in society against those of big business.

|| Make Precarious Employment Illegal ||

As we have discussed, precarious employment is ever more common, especially for women, with almost 120,000 people in Scotland currently on zero hour contracts. The failure to guarantee hours leaves women insecure, unable to plan ahead with money or time. Other forms of precarious work, such as casual or temporary contracts or abusive probationary periods, are also increasing and can leave workers without basic labour rights such as holiday or sick pay.

Glasgow University students and trade unions began a campaign against zero-hour contracts at the university in 2013: this powerful example could be generalised across workforces in Scotland, acting as a base for the full illegalisation of zero-hour contracts and other forms of precarious employment that control women's lives.

|| Tax the Rich, Not the Poor ||

The White Paper names control of the tax system as a major benefit of independence, but their only concrete proposal is lowering corporate tax. We reject this idea. Instead we argue for a progressive tax system where those who benefit the most (including corporations as well as individuals) should pay the most back into the system. Higher income tax for the rich is a basic democratic demand.

Beyond this we also propose reducing VAT, the sales tax, and basing the tax system on income. VAT disproportionately affects those on lower incomes, therefore more women, as it does not distinguish between consumers. Slashing or eliminating VAT and increasing higher rate income tax can help redistribute the taxation burden.

|| COMMUNITY GENDER BUDGETING ||

The Scottish Women's Gender Budget Group currently carries out important work analysing the gendered impact of government public policy. This has often helped expose the current system's bias against women. However, this happens at an elite level and focuses on pushing the government to make small changes that incrementally assist women. Can we go further and have gender budgeting at a community level?

Gendered budgeting – specifically tailored to empower women to solve chronic problems of poverty, abuse and social disintegration – can be introduced in stages, the better for relayed experience to inform the more comprehensive and national development of such schemes.

By experimenting on a Scottish city, such as Glasgow, a central fund taken from general taxation could be administered by local committees of women. This could set up projects for everything from the economic uplift of women with bursaries and zero interest loans to infrastructure for protecting women from domestic violence such as refuges and drop-in centres. These would have professional staff trained to counsel and advise women in violent and otherwise dangerous relationships.

Such facilities would link to broader networks for Scotland's social and economic renaissance, and as such would be part of the public sector funded with state money. But crucially they would be democratic and organised by women in their own communities: they would meld state and civic society, volunteer and professional activity, promoting new forms of social activism and civic solidarity.

| | LAND REFORM | |

Most commentators bemoan Scotland's miserable land ownership record, which is Europe's most concentrated. What's less acknowledged is the thoroughly gendered nature of our antiquated order. Incredibly, Scotland's land inheritance laws still privilege the oldest male heir to the estate.

This property system, known as primogeniture, is a feudal relic with no place in the 21st century. Moreover, what are euphemistically called "family estates", supposedly ownership by whole families, are in fact owned by the family's male head and eventual male successor. It's merely a disguise for the complete lack of women land owners.

One way to deal with this problem would be to bring the legal rights of inheritance of children up to date in order to afford them a legal dispensation without reference to bronze-age patriarchal practices. But inheritance itself is a barrier to equality between the genders and to equality full stop.

As well as taking the proverbial chainsaw to Scotland's outmoded laws, we should also resolve to split up the large estates altogether. Local communities and national agencies could then dispense with it for useful purposes, such as developing renewable energy, nature reserves, house building and so on. Special co-ordination with women's committees could see that this redivision of the estates would serve the interests of, and be brought under the administration of, women in both rural communities and across the nation as a whole.

|| End Methodological Bias ||

Measuring gross domestic product (GDP) continues to be the dominant way to measure the wealth of a country. As we have discussed above, this excludes much of the work of women as well as not including wider indicators of socio-economic wellbeing such as gender equality.

We propose that Scotland adopts alternative forms of measuring economic performance: many already exist such as the Gender Empowerment Index which incorporates women's participation in paid work, managerial jobs and parliamentary seats. Unfortunately, at the moment this tends to measure elite women's involvement and therefore shows bias in the overall progression of women. But some similar measure could prove effective.

A crucial concern is how care hours are divided between genders: so alongside measuring women's improvement in the paid sphere, we must assess men's role in the caring and household sphere. This is where much inequality originates. Of course, changing measurement is not itself change. But it can help re-visualise the economy and what we value within it.

|| Socialisation of Care ||

Can we imagine a world where paid workers not individuals do domestic work? Where children could be cared for communally as well as individually? The idea of housework and caring duties as the private duty of the individual is so ingrained in our society that these ideas can appear radical, even utopian.

Instead, can we see this for what it is: an antiquated relic of a decaying social system? The privatisation of household work and care work is not necessary nor is it the most "natural" way to organise society. Can we question why one section of the population – women – should end up with the responsibility for something that we all require?

There are alternative ways in which society could function. Responsibility for household tasks and many aspects of care work could be part of a social state: tasks such as cooking and cleaning would be done by paid workers. Those who enjoyed these tasks would be free to do them, but it would not be as part of a required time-compressing drudgery nor would it be inherently gendered. When we talk about reinvestment in welfare, can we keep an eye on these wider possibilities?

We have a base to build on. Alongside the expansion of the current childcare proposals a massive and sustained investment into a new care industry could, coupled with new green industries, issue in an economic and social revival in Scotland.

With tens of thousands of new skilled care workers employed on regular hours contracts the decline in care standards across the UK can be reversed. This need not take the form of a massive expansion in retirement home type accommodation. Rather, the new outlays of care workers, many of whom would be specialists able to deal with specific mental or physical health needs, could mainly operate a home visit service with the freedoms and dignity of the elderly and disabled restored. If this is coupled with an increasingly confident women workforce, the pressure can build for a more sustained change towards that of full socialisation of care and domestic work.

|| PROCESS TO POWER ||

Unequal pay begins when women start their adult lives and grows during the life cycle. And yes, men are doing more chores and childcare – but not much more, and much less than women. According to time-use surveys of thousands of households over three decades, men's dedicated childcare rose at a rate of about 30 seconds per day, per year. Their contribution to housework rose at a rate of one minute per day, per year. Change is palpable, but pitiful.

The ideas here are suggestions not a manifesto. There are many and varied demands which could improve life for women and start to build economic power. A final question remains: how do we make such demands part of the independence campaign? And how do we use them to build into deeper demands and ultimately a transfer of power from men to women, from owner to worker? The way forward will involve different aspects of radical and feminist civil society, new social movements, and, of course, trade unions.

Trade unions remain crucial to workers' economic, political and social power, by building collective organisation and by taking democratic action to improve living standards. However, union rights have been under continual attack in the neoliberal period, and things will get radically worse if, as looks increasingly likely, the Tories win in 2015. Cameron has pledged "a whole range of measures" to further restrict trade unions and the rights of workers, while Labour remains at best silent on the issue. Under Westminster workers' rights will only get worse. The UK has the second most restrictive anti trade union legislation in Europe. Freedom to organise at work is a basic human right, which the UK insists on curbing, and this hurts society as a whole. But, like any anti-democratic law, it also has a particular effect on women.

As explained, many women get trapped in a cycle of poorly paid precarious work. Yes, there might be more women in the boardroom, but those forced to top up chronic low-pay with credit cards, tax credits or universal credit, are much more numerous. And as such, we think this is worthy of at least as much discussion. The work that women do – hospitality, cleaning, care – faces severe issues. During the independence debate, discussions centre on "jobs for the boys", the implications for shipbuilding and military industries if we vote Yes. By contrast, nobody is talking about jobs done by women that have been outsourced, cut or privatised. The public sector was always women's best chance of equal pay, but now privatisation constantly threatens. The reason public sector work had the best chance of equal pay, was, of course, because of its high trade union density. Independence is the only way to fix this.

We are now living in an increasingly privatised economy, where unionisation is less that 30% and low-pay, bonus culture and zero hour contracts are endemic. These are industrial factors which promote inequality and hierarchies. Continuing with this type of industrial culture *will* grow the gender pay gap. Women can benefit the most from better industrial democracy.

Of course, trade unions must change to reshape an independent Scotland. In 2008, then-general secretary of Unite, Derek Simpson as part of his "British Jobs for British Workers" campaign, posed with two Union Jack-bikinied page 3 models. Not exactly the vision of progressive trade unionism that we would wish to see. Despite much progression since 2008, they haven't shaken the pale, male, and stale model. Frances O'Grady, the new female TUC leader, highlights the need for radical transformation across the board in terms of gender equality.

The women who clean schools, work in hospitals, teach children, care for our elderly, and care for their own children are the backbone of our society, and we need a "new trade unionism" which reflects this. They need participatory organising strategies that empower workers at the base, not force them into a deferential trade union hierarchy. By using organising models which encourage collectivity, collective action and real workers' democracy, we can begin this process. However, this will still be within the confines of the anti-trade union laws, until we can break with Westminster. There is no chance of developing a new industrial relations policy which rebalances the power between workers and bosses, women and men until the current constitutional arrangement.

A socially-just independence must abolish the anti-trade union laws and allow the right to strike on political grounds. The criminalisation of solidarity action is anti-democratic and also has a particularly bad effect on women: given our concentration in disparate and precarious work, sometimes solidarity with other workplaces is our most effective weapon. Collective bargaining at the sectoral or beyond that at the societal level removes the power from individual employers to drive wages down.

The White Paper recognises both the importance of collective bargaining and the right for workers to be represented on company boards. This is an important step and trade unionists should use it to push for more powers for workers to control decision making. Nonetheless, we must be aware that workers' representation can be mainly symbolic, and risks incorporating a few figures to legitimise management decisions.

For this reason, unions should use independence as an opportunity to reenergise members and reengage with working class politics, instead of mere service provision. The unions have an image as "male, pale and stale", and they must improve women's representation, by quotas if necessary. Even filling top positions with women won't be enough. Instead, unions must transform their philosophy to incorporate the work women do and to challenge society's undervaluation of it. This can rejuvenate the trade union movement at its grassroots, while also raising women's status as industrial and political leaders from below.

Recent strike activity in the UK has seen support and "solidarity action" from anti-austerity groups and political movements. This illustrates how the above demands could work through and with social movements and unions, strengthening one another. However, it also outlines the importance of the right to protest in freedom, without violent crackdowns on those merely exercising democratic rights. This goes hand in hand with an end to mass surveillance.

Women in Scotland must seize this chance to change how workers are valued. Westminster offers nothing for collective workers' power: only with independence can we build on current proposals. We stand in solidarity with workers in the rest of the UK, but Scotland has the chance to offer a way forward.

|| CONCLUSION ||

Independence is the beginning of this vision, not the end. We have outlined the reality for women in Scotland today under neoliberalism: changing women's constitutional power is just one factor in this. However, independence provides an opening to build on the challenge to Britain's right-wing consensus.

The current devolution settlement constrains a genuine discussion about Scotland's political differences. Successive Scottish governments can engage in left-sounding posturing merely by mitigating the extreme excesses of British neoliberalism. Only a Yes vote can force us beyond this and allow us to build on the gains of Scotland relative to the rest of the UK.

This can be used to improve life for women at the expense of the system, gaining concessions in improved welfare and support organisations for women. However, we have tried to push beyond this argument: in a global economy we need to begin the process of building our own power as women, one that comes from below. This does not need to start with radical demands, but it must end with radical conclusions.

7

POWER AND EQUALITY

|| INTRODUCTION ||

With the global financial system teetering, worldwide production and employment in freefall, and the looming prospect of a prolonged recession, capitalist crisis supplies the inescapable backdrop for every serious attempt at critical theory. Henceforth, feminist theorists cannot avoid the question of capitalist society. Large-scale social theory, aimed at clarifying the nature and roots of crisis, as well as the prospects for an emancipatory resolution, promises to regain its place in feminist thought. **Nancy Fraser.**

The devolved Scottish parliament has allowed more representation for women, at least compared to Westminster's woeful record. But progress has stalled, even declining slightly since 1999. Independence by itself won't solve the crisis of women's participation in public life, but it creates new opportunities to transform political institutions.

The No campaign insist that Scotland already "has the best of both worlds"; but in gender-terms, this is laughable. Just over a third of Holyrood MSPs are women, a poor figure; but Westminster, just 22 percent female, lags even further behind. Better Together has been silent on women's representation: even "Women Together" has not a single policy proposal, and their campaign role is largely emblematic.

How can anyone take parliament seriously, when they scarcely consult half the population? These are not merely questions of equality *per se*, but also of equal access to power, which is integral to social justice. Britain styles itself as a "modern democracy", yet only 4 of 23 cabinet members are women. In the global league table of women's representation the UK ranks 58th. When politicians make welfare, defence and other policies, half the electorate barely counts; and of course, the same applies to BME, working class, and LGBT communities. This normalises white, male and privileged leadership in society.

This problem runs deeper than the Con-Dems. A recent New Statesman article, titled, "What Labour's Red Princes tell us about Britain", shows how Labour selects candidates from increasingly narrow careerist elites. The research found more than half the party's candidates in marginal or inherited seats have already worked in politics or think tanks. Nepotism and cronyism means passing influence from male patron to male protégé; and in many areas of ruling class life, from politics to finance, it's growing. Patronage is the most ancient and directly "patriarchal" form of social power relation, and it bypasses women. In this sense, both state and civil society are "gendered". The ideals of parliamentary democracy face true crisis, with a few dynastic families competing for power, as fathers handing down the right to rule to sons.

|| DEVOLUTION ||

While Scotland is no paradise, devolution did help women to engage in politics. Before it, feminists and trade unionists in Scottish civil society campaigned for equal rights and access to power. In 1989 the STUC women's committee presented base points for a "new politics" in Scotland, calling for family friendly hours, childcare facilities, and a mainstreaming of equal opportunities in Parliament.

But the most innovative proposal was equal representation of men and women in Holyrood, the 50/50 campaign. Building support from across Scottish society, the Women's Co-ordination Group forced Scottish Labour and the Scottish Liberal Democrats to agree to gender balance mechanisms in the parliament. The first election in 1999 saw more women elected to Holyrood (37%) than had ever gained election for Scottish (or any other) seats at Westminster.

Since then, the record has been one of "stalling not falling", although in truth women's representation has fallen slightly in some areas. Progress hasn't entirely collapsed, but hasn't been built on either. Various issues are to blame, but the likeliest cause is internal selection processes in Scottish parties. Few made serious intellectual strides on gender. But, beyond this, Scotland as a whole should take responsibility for these failures, and assuming our parliament is always better for women would be complacent.

In 1999, a consensus demanded "new politics" in Scotland, and we do that again, and more. Too often in the referendum, we're constrained by old expectations of what leadership looks like, what power looks like, and representation means. In this campaign, we need a new political revolution, which goes beyond token women in formal positions, and reaches down into everyday life.

The only threat to elite power is citizens' and workers' power. While we should not capitulate to Westminster, nor should we aspire to recreate cliques, scions, and cabals in Holyrood. Many liberal feminists were too uncritical in welcoming Devolution's "new politics". Although we accept aggressive, macho cultures and family unfriendly policies have been barriers in the past, tackling only them doesn't stop the problem's roots. Undoubtedly, the Houses of Parliament have normalised sexist culture – Mike Hancock and Lord Rennard's behaviour comes to mind – and there's a need for practical alternatives. But unless this involves broader societal and economic change, permanent progress is not certain.

|| SUBSTANTIAL EQUALITY ||

We've written this book because an independent Scotland needn't repeat the failures of the past: there are opportunities to go further and do better. But we shouldn't imagine putting women in politics improves everyone's lives. For instance, despite austerity's brutal impact on women, Labour's shadow Work and Pensions secretary, Rachel Reeves, promises tougher welfare policies than the Tories. While the Iraq War has "set Iraqi women back seventy years" (see chapter 3), many still hail Hilary Clinton, a cheerleader for invasion, as a feminist icon. Of course, these individuals aren't to blame for cuts and wars. But they show that simply clearing the road for women in political leadership won't change the social fabric of capitalist patriarchy. While neoliberalism and imperialism continue to shape our institutions, women's lot as a whole won't improve.

For us, abstract equality is not the end goal. Changing existing institutions, like parliament and so on, is crucial to picturing women's power. However, deep-seated inequalities aren't so easily shifted, and thus empowering some always means disempowering others. For example, if privileged women gain election, unpaid housework, low wages, and oppression will continue further down the ladder. Our end goal should be women's liberation and democratic socialism; an equal parliament is merely a means.

A recent Westminster example demonstrates why these distinctions matter. The new Conservative women's minister, Nicky Morgan, has hinted they will consider all-women shortlists for the 2015 elections: the real problem, she said, was "not enough women... coming forward". This met with an immediate backlash from traditionalists. Ann Widdecombe, a Tory grandee, criticised the moves because "neither Margaret Thatcher nor I needed this kind of help to get into parliament". In their eyes, inequality, by implication, was largely the fault of individual women, lacking initiative and ambition.

Whether the Tories can beat this internal resistance is debatable. But a more fundamental point remains: the Conservative party is anti-women, no matter who it elects. Since 2010, they have cut child benefits, attacked women's status and earnings as carers, and hammered public sector workers with pay freezes and privatisation. Morgan's predecessor, Maria Miller, openly stated her preference for reducing the legal limit for abortion from 24 weeks to 20. Theresa May and David Cameron (in a "personal capacity", of course) backed these moves. Health Secretary, Jeremy Hunt, responsible for flogging NHS England and Wales to Virgin Healthcare, gave his own view. "12 weeks is the right point for it," he said. So, we've got Government ministers, both men and women, openly attacking women's bodies and economic security.

Thatcher waged economic and social war on women with equal ferocity. One woman's success within a corrupt, archaic and patriarchal order won't guarantee progress for all women. As feminists, we favour women's empowerment: but we're against giving anyone power to seize the rights of others, as Tories do. And here lies the problem: simply placing women in influential positions doesn't bring equality between genders. Feminism is not a question of biological sex, but a matter of ideology.

|| THATCHER'S LEGACY ||

Thatcher's legacy is part of central Scotland's entrenched ideology: for Dennis Canavan, she "changed the face of Scotland". Others recognise her paradoxical role as a driving force behind Scottish independence, having "treated the people of Scotland with absolute contempt", again in Canavan's words.

And thus, when the media announced her death, hundreds of Glaswegians assembled in George Square, as they always said they would. The street party celebrated "people's history": the miners and their families from the 1984-5 strike, the Irish hunger strikers, and the stoicism of Scotland's working class. Sadly, in contrast to the mood of the street celebrations, an out-pouring of sexism occurred online, describing Thatcher as a "witch", a "bitch" and an "old dog". Like other women in politics, Thatcher faced constant misogynistic abuse while in power: about her dress, her body, her looks, her mannerisms. No matter how odious her policies, this is unworthy of our cause. We reject any criticisms of Thatcher that reflect inherently sexist attitudes. Nonetheless, we must continually re-state that Margaret Thatcher is no feminist icon, and history must never be re-written that way. She grasped power when the women's movement was strong, but rejected both its goals and its methods. To quote broadcaster and journalist, Bidisha:

> She likes what macho, sexist, patriarchal men have always liked: war, the defence of the status quo, established power, entrenched inequality, heavily-rigged individualist competition and absolute freedom. Not freedom as in emancipation, but the greedy savagery of an unregulated market in which man eats man and woman is neither seen nor heard.

Again, this highlights the dangers of divorcing class from gender representation. Margaret Thatcher didn't merely ignore patriarchy: her market-driven, imperialist politics pushed women back, making public life more unreachable. More worryingly, she created a damaging precedent, which says, women have no real barriers in politics, as long as their chauvinism equals the most jingoistic, sexist males. Just like America's Sarah Palin, her example has nothing to offer our movement.

|| THE SEDUCTION OF FEMINISM ||

Thatcher doesn't represent women' aspirations, she represents neoliberalism. This term means a "grab-bag of ideas, based on the fundamentalist notion that markets are self-correcting, allocate resources efficiently and serve the public well", in the words of Nobel prize winning economist Joseph Stiglitz. Neoliberals insist that any notion of "public good" is misleading; instead, they see public services as deductions from individual welfare.

Critiques of neoliberalism show a vile legacy of record inequalities, financial instability and environmental crisis. Other studies note that its "gender-blind" doctrines cannot account for gender differences and inequalities. Neoliberal policies often have a markedly negative effect on women; and pro-market politicians, especially Thatcher, single-out vulnerable groups like single mothers for cuts and scapegoating.

But there's a deeper danger here, because neoliberalism also damaged feminist engagement with politics, and the public's appreciation of feminism. In a study of British and German women aged 18-35, two broad patterns emerged. First, they recognised feminism as valuable, but anachronistic, and therefore irrelevant to everyday life. The second, more interesting, feature was how they framed feminism in terms of an individualist ideology. They often rejected the need for collectivism, instead identifying themselves as autonomous agents who could negotiate market society for their own ends.

So individualist cultures have undermined the collective power built up by women's movements. They've also reinforced psychological insecurity, by enforcing a culture of winners and losers. Failure reflects the defects of individuals, who flunk life's tests because they won't maximise the advantages of their resources. A glimpse of hope exists in the reappearance of feminism but there is work to be done in linking the progressive edges of this upsurge to a broader political change.

As Thatcher rose to prominence, she "pulled the ladder up" after her. Tokenistic changes to power's appearance can leave oppression intact, unless they challenge the social roots of inequality. In recent decades, feminism has flipped between rebuilding women's collective power and encouraging individual women to achieve market success. Under neoliberalism, there are more women in boardrooms (albeit still very few), but beyond these cosmetic changes, the fabric of feminism has shattered. British parliamentary traditions and neoliberal politics have worked hand-in-hand to incorporate female elites and undermine collectivist, emancipatory politics.

|| NEOLIBERAL CAPTURE ||

Neoliberal institutions, from the Bank of England to the IMF, take little interest in feminism, nor the finer points of "gender issues". But in recent years they have undoubtedly refocused on women's role in economic development.

Of course, empowerment and women's agency play no part in their deliberations: neoliberals want institutions to feminise investment because it is "smart economics". The result, far from emancipation, is a toxic mix of overwork and cheap labour, leading to the "feminisation of poverty" (see chapter 6). Neoliberals claim to offer consumers absolute sovereignty, thus raising women's "agency"; but proximity to markets means harsher exposure to all society's oppressions. Private sector jobs, for instance, almost always have a bigger gender pay gap, more bullying, and less protection from sexism and abuse.

For socialist feminists today, there is ever greater anxiety about feminism's "entanglement" with neoliberal efforts to build a "free society", in which markets replace everything (education, healthcare, social security). "During the last two decades, most [feminists] kept their distance from the sort of large-scale social theorizing associated with Marxism," warns Nancy Fraser. "The critique of capitalist society…all but vanished from the feminist agenda." Feminist priorities shifted from social solidarity to celebrating careerism: from highlighting interdependence, to encouraging meritocracy. Feminism has been uprooted from its origins as a collective project, by neoliberal, corporate and third sector emphasis on individual empowerment and "choice", particularly through misappropriation of a well-known feminist phrase: "the personal is political". Journalist Rahila Gupta writes,

["The personal is political"] resulted from joining up the dots between individual women's experiences …[and] systematic inequality, which needed collective effort to dismantle. However, this same principle is broad enough to allow business interests to ride on its back.

Our sense of collective struggle gives our movement strength, but neoliberal Britain has shattered it.

| | FEMINISM'S BROADER RESPONSIBILITIES | |

Subjugating women's needs and women's bodies will continue at Westminster regardless of its gender-balance, reflecting the deep roots of oppression. But also, liberal feminism has also forgotten our deeper responsibilities to other oppressed groups marginalised by mainstream parties. This is another reason successful "role models" cannot liberate all women. Oppressions overlap and entangle with one another, and only by collective effort can we achieve liberation.

Token representation is not real power. But even the latter is insufficient without resistance, which is empowerment's twin. Feminism is rudderless unless it demands redistribution of wealth, challenges market fundamentalism, and defends national ownership. These substantive policies of empowerment are anathema to neoliberals. And thus, wherever women take to the streets, or organise against austerity, the authoritarian, anti-feminist core of these institutions asserts itself. "Empowering women" cannot be top-down, it must build agency from below.

While we've shown that British democracy privileges men over women, race and class oppression are equally important. That is why, for this chapter's last section, we outline an alternative vision of politics under independence, in which women – working class women in particular – can shape a truly different Scotland. We'll also consider political agency's role in bringing emancipation back into feminist politics.

| | PARTICIPATORY ALTERNATIVES | |

Participatory budgeting (PB) began in the 1980s, as an attempt to alleviate vast inequalities in the Brazilian city of Porto Alegre, where over a third of citizens had no clean water, health care, or education. The experiment has been remarkably successful, and offers important lessons for feminists and radicals in Scotland.

At its simplest, PB gives ordinary citizens direct democratic control of how councils disburse public money. Porto Alegre residents meet in neighbourhood, regional, and city-wide assemblies, together with elected politicians, to debate priorities and vote on spending decisions.

As well as empowering destitute communities and giving oppressed groups a voice, the process forces politicians to meet their obligations to their constituents. Participatory budgeting promotes democratic and transparent administration of resources and reduces corruption and the mishandling of public funds. It encourages public investment towards society's most pressing needs for the benefit of the greatest number of people.

Bolivia's 1994 Law of Popular Participation, a similar case, gave municipal councils power to design and implement local development policies and programmes, with finance transferred from central government. Community organisations led five-year municipal plans, and were given autonomous control over areas. They were assigned rights and duties over social, infrastructure and environmental matters. Residents set up Vigilance Committees to act as watchdogs, ensuring that community projects and priorities were reflected in their budgets and expenditure.

PB still reflects external inequalities in society, such as gender, and thus it is no sovereign remedy. However, there are examples of how gender, if put at the centre of PB, can "count women in".

The case of Recife, again in Brazil, highlights how gender can be integrated into PB models. Their model not only included area or neighbourhood meetings to decide budget priorities, but also "thematic" forums, including one on women. This was a specific space for women to discuss not only the issues affecting them directly and the priorities that they thought should be budgeted for, but how PB should operate across Recife. These discussions prompted three initiatives:

1. Recife provided mobile play areas for children at meetings to help women with childcare responsibilities participate in budgeting.

2. The participants actively went out and campaigned to encourage local women's participation in PB meetings.

3. The PB group met with government officials and women activists to enhance participation. This led to the production of pamphlets and music for community radio stations.

These initiatives brought some improvements in terms of participation. By 2004, women represented 57 percent of those participating in Recife's forums. Representation at managerial and strategic levels, where women's visibility was poorer, proved more difficult: only 45 percent of those were women. Clearly, though, these are huge figures compared to Scotland.

We think by using similar practices, allowing ordinary people in Scotland to actively govern themselves, and to allow the mainstreaming of gender issues, we could significantly redress so-called political dis-engagement. These would be clear spaces for women's participation and agency. So, as opposed to a Westminster old boy network, we would actively encourage practical involvement at a level anyone can understand. If this works in Brazil and Bolivia, confronting huge legacies of endemic poverty, it can work here.

Beyond this, an independent Scotland offers new hope for constitutional radicalism. One idea is to establish

SCOTTISH INDEPENDENCE: A FEMINIST RESPONSE

a Women's Assembly, made up of elected representatives or delegates from local community councils. This would enhance women's skills as leaders, as policy-designers, as political operators, but retain links to grassroots activism. Any decision on Social Security, on Childcare, on Education, on the public sector – any political decision which disproportionately affects women – should have to pass through the Women's Assembly before becoming law.

This type of second chamber is hardly far-fetched. For centuries, British legislation passed through a second chamber "elected" by landed birthright and privilege. Why not a women's parliament instead?

|| The Thatcher Effect ||

In this chapter, we've shown the crisis of women's representation in UK politics. And, to be clear, we absolutely support any measures to get more women into politics, including but not limited to 50:50 quotas, and to have a more gender representative democracy. This does change the way in which other women look at political power, and question their own access to it. But Scotland faces particular "democratic deficits" that take us back, once again, to Thatcher's legacy.

Polls show that working class Scots are far likelier to vote Yes in 2014 than anyone else. But women are among the least likely to vote Yes. We believe this reflects deep-rooted contradictions in the independence campaign. Much of the independence movement is powered by an anti-Thatcher legacy, the SSP, the poll tax and so on. As we've outlined in this chapter, certain aspects of feminism were co-opted by neoliberal institutions and how aspects of liberal feminism foster a feminism that is, if not outright neoliberal, then at least individualist. There is, under neoliberalism, a concurrent failure to build a collective feminism, one that can engage politically in independence debates. Instead it means isolated women must "battle it out" not just against patriarchy, but against each other, for the glories of personal enrichment, the only sure sign of self-worth. Those who must fall back on collectivism, it follows, are failures. Those who mention oppression are losers, and their weakness is at fault, not the system.

Our feminist case for independence faces this contradiction. Working class women are overlooked in politics as we know it. It is no surprise that they have been overlooked by the official Yes campaign and liberal feminists. This is not a story of blame, but to recognise that women from working class background will continue to be overlooked, unless we vote Yes. Independence is no panacea, but it provides us with the only opportunity to connect back the power of women's struggle as a collective struggle in opposition to the current neoliberal settlement. This involves exposing the limits of the current Scottish system for women and thinking about how to transform our society. To seek equality for women under the current neoliberal order means seeking out equality that relies on other women's inequality, be that through race, class, sexuality and so on. And thus, we must have a binary approach to putting what might be deemed "women's issues" on the table. We want more women in power: but to accompany this we absolutely must have the ability to organise women at a grassroots level, in opposition to neoliberalism. If we cannot, we face replicating and reproducing the same inequalities over and over again.

A Yes vote can restore the power of a women's collective struggle, and through this we can transform our society to be more egalitarian and representative. A Yes vote means overcoming shame in collectivism and solidarity. The pressure for this change must come from the bottom: a feminism from below.

8

CONCLUSION

Our case for Yes is both reasonable and revolutionary.

Feminism needs to reimagine the independence debate. Vague promises of change, fairness and equality provide nothing for women particularly in an age when Louise Mensch makes the ludicrous statement that the Tories are "relentlessly focused on social justice". The language of liberation has been absorbed by the establishment while the message has not.

The Yes campaign has faltered on the question of gender. Women know that "change" if it does not explicitly include women usually means "change for men". The question of childcare, while welcome, shows precisely what is wrong: it's very framing as a "women's issue" is a problem. We need to develop an analysis that questions why our lives are still structured by antiquated gender stereotypes.

We have attempted here to engage with the reality of women's lives in Scotland and Scotland as part of the UK: the history that surrounds us, the cultures we grow up in, our access to work, being a woman in a military society and our ability to redress the imbalance of power. For us, these issues are all linked together in a history of domination by Empire, a culture where women come second, a hegemonic economic doctrine that punishes women, an obsession with military power, and systems of government which consistently shut women out. We see independence as breaking away from these realities, opening the door for a different type of society.

We have our concerns about the SNP model for a future Scotland, particularly for women. However, the opposition to the Westminster consensus can be used to find alternative pathways. This book is not a manifesto nor is it a definitive work for feminists in Scotland but rather aims to provide ideas for systematic change. This depends on a re-democratised and political feminist movement. We have a strong feminist tradition to pull on and an emerging youth feminism that is already focused on exposing old power relations.

Our critique of the current economic, social and political system aims to expose the reality for women in the UK, a reality that goes down to the roots of how our society functions. Ultimately, this involves talking about class; it is here that we distinguish ourselves from the other feminist publications we have mentioned. The problem of reorganisation of labour between the household and the paid workplace is not one of will; it is one of opposing interests between labour and capital as well as men and women, which is of course also deeply racialised.

Mainstreaming exists in a paradox. The problem with the current political system is not that mainstreaming has not been implemented fully; it is that our institutions are the embodiment of male privilege. They will concede a gender mainstreaming agenda formally if forced, and use it to legitimise themselves. But they cannot support a gender equal outcome.

We are living in dangerous times. We are living in what Beatrix Campbell neatly describes as a "neoliberal neo-patriarchy." Our society is happy for its girls to aspire to become doctors, astronauts, or even prime minister. But when it comes to genuine, real and radical reforms of the sexual division of labour, all avenues for change close up in front of us. Neoliberalism destroys social settlements, the public good and the power of the collective in favour of the markets, privatisation and the untold rights of the individual.

This new settlement is the enemy of women, and it is the enemy of feminism because it abandons the very source of the power for changing society for women; our social solidarity and security. Feminism dies as these things, which are its life source, are cut off. Our feminism is then used as rhetoric to justify invading other nations, for selling us shower gels, to bomb Muslim women, to keep rape convictions low, to sell us vibrators, to boost TV ratings, to make us hate other women.

Along with every other social solidarity, our language of liberation has been traded on the markets, and sold back to us, neatly packaged. Because of this, there will be women who do not recognise the realities we describe in this book. But they will surely recognise this: the gap between men's and women's money, time, power, respect and access to resources is getting larger year on year.

Britain is typical of neo-liberal neo-patriarchy: it is an archaic and masculine state. We think that there women should vote Yes as a matter of urgency. Britain is inseparable from its neoliberal institutions, which have systematically shattered and dismantled any sense of collective struggle for women's equality. Britain has duped women into thinking they've won some concessions for equality, but it has in reality set us back.

Breaking up Britain can help stop this trajectory, and it opens up a tiny crack for new struggles to ferment, and for new radical victories. By using some of the reforms set out in this book, we think that women can be empowered in their everyday lives, to take on new challenges and new battles. A Yes vote means the creation of new institutions for a new state: a new media, a new legal system, a new economy, and of course, a new parliament. We must shape these institutions, to dramatically and radically change how our society looks and functions.

Women are at the centre of all demands for a new type of egalitarian society. And a new type of egalitarian society is one which, at its foundation, gives equal respect to women's time, labour, bodies and access to power.